PAUL GASCOIGNE

THE INSIDE STORY

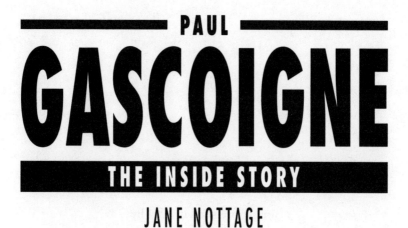

PAUL
GASCOIGNE
THE INSIDE STORY

JANE NOTTAGE

CollinsWillow
An Imprint of HarperCollins*Publishers*

First published in 1993 by
CollinsWillow
an imprint of HarperCollins*Publishers*

© Jane Nottage, 1993

**A CIP catalogue record for this book
is available from the British Library**

ISBN 0 00 218537 7

Printed in Great Britain by
Butler & Tanner Ltd

Colour plate section credits:
Allsport, Bob Thomas Sports Photography, Dufoto,
Foto Calzuola, Fotosports International, Jane Nottage
and Syndication International

CONTENTS

This book is dedicated to two people.

Peter Stewart managing editor of *World Soccer, Shoot, Soccer Stars and 90 Minutes*, who gave me my first break in soccer journalism, and who has been my guardian angel ever since.

And my boyfriend Massimo Gerri, whose patience, love and advice have seen me through the long days and nights of writing this biography.

ACKNOWLEDGEMENTS

There are many people who have helped me in my quest to present the definitive picture of Paul Gascoigne. They include my parents, Margaret and Geoffrey Nottage, who have always given me their wholehearted support; Jeff Powell, a friend and respected adviser; Grancarlo Galavotti, soccer expert from *La Gazzetta dello Sport*; Alberto dalla Palma of *Il Corriere dello Sport*; Bruno Bartolozzi; Gabriele de Bari of *Il Messeggero*; Carlo Regalia, ex-general manager of Lazio Football Club; Glenn and Faith Roeder, who are the living proof that there are some really nice people in the world; Bobby Robson, whose enthusiasm took us to almost the pinnacle of the world; Graham Taylor, whose dedication to Gascoigne was rewarded with moments of genius and great frustration; Terry Venables, who in spite of his own troubles always found time to talk to me; Gary and Michelle Lineker and Stephanie Moore for their friendship; Paul's family for their support and friendship; my solicitor, Andrew Green for his advice and patience; the people at HarperCollins, especially Sheila Crowley for introducing me to everyone; Editorial Director, Michael Doggart; Tom Whiting, who spent sleepless nights editing the book; Deborah Kayser, designer Rachel Smyth and Juliet Annan. Others to thank include Colin Moynihan, whose wisdom has helped me see things more clearly; Lazio Football Club who have always been sympathetic and supportive during the difficult times, and in particular; and Enrico Bendoni, a friend from Italia '90. I would like to wish Lazio Chairman, Sergio Cragnotti, all the best for the 1993/94 season and hope his faith in the genius of 'Gazza' will be rewarded. And a special thank you to Toni Damascelli, and Antonio Matarrese, chairman of the Italian Football Federation, for his friendship and insight into the world of Italian football.

Finally, thanks to everyone connected to the great game of 'calcio' for producing the most exciting, entertaining spectacle in the world.

Jane Nottage
July 1993

INTRODUCTION

P aul Gascoigne is one of the most controversial sportsmen on the international scene. Love him or hate him, it is impossible to ignore him. He is the topic of discussion, not only in his native Gateshead, but all over the world. You can't help but admire his skills and determination in overcoming an injury that would have put most people out of the game of football, just as you can't help but be exasperated by some of his off-pitch antics. Yet how many people can say they really know Paul Gascoigne, or 'Gazza', as he is more affectionately known? Although loud and showy, he is also very private and surprisingly fragile. He has a soft heart but a selfish streak, he is generous yet pernickety. In other words he is an enigma. Even his best friends do not know what to expect next.

Gazza first came to my attention during England's 1990 World Cup campaign in Italy. Until then, he had been a half-conscious shadow in the general melee of the football world. By the time Gazza had emerged from his chrysalis to become an international football celebrity, I had already been working in Italy for nearly five years, initially as a journalist for *Shoot* and *World Soccer*, then on my first novel *The Italians* before joining Italia '90, the World Cup organizing committee, which is where our paths first crossed.

Through my involvement with Italian football, I had met many of the outstanding talents that Italy attracts. In Milan,

I spent a lot of time trying to gain an insight into the game by listening to people like Liam Brady, Karlheinz Rummenigge, Alessandro Altobelli and Marco Tardelli, all of whom were highly successful players. Both Liam and Karlheinz had proved themselves to be not only outstanding players, but also very professional in their approach to living and playing in another country. They had learnt the language, applied their skills to Serie A – the premier league of Italian football – and adapted to the demands of being superstars in a country crazy about football or 'calcio'. In particular, Liam will always be remembered for his professionalism in scoring from the penalty spot for his club Juventus, shortly after the club had told him he was to be sold to make way for Michel Platini.

I had also followed closely the Ian Rush saga at Juventus, which had seen one of Britain's top strikers destroyed and demoralized after only a year in Italy. Ian, unlike Gazza, is rather an introverted character and suffered from the insensitive attitude that Juventus adopted towards him. Like Gazza he was purchased a year before arriving in Italy to play, and he too made very little progress with the language, but his failure lay more at the hands of the club than with him. So when I knew that Lazio wanted to buy Gazza, I was curious as to how it would all work out.

After the World Cup, Gazza went home a celebrity and left many Italians wondering if he could be successful in Italy. It wasn't long before several clubs started to make enquiries about buying him. At first Tottenham were adamant in their refusal to sell him, but their dire financial state forced them at least to consider the £5 million offer made by Italian club Lazio to bring him to Rome.

It was when Lazio expressed an interest in Gazza that I became involved with his advisers, solicitor Mel Stein and accountant Len Lazarus, flying with them to Rome to attend their first meeting with Lazio chairman Gianmarco Calleri, general manager Carlo Regali and team manager Maurizio Manzini. It was the start of a long period of negotiation during which Gazza injured his knee twice and both clubs changed hands, but finally in the summer of 1992 England's most gifted footballer was transferred to Lazio .

Once the deal was agreed, I became Gazza's personal assistant and commercial consultant in Italy. We flew to Rome in August 1991, March 1992 and then May 1992 for the final fitness tests and each time I was at his side to ease him through the transition period and help sort out any problems.

Gazza is a lovable character but not the most organized of people and once we arrived in Italy, the role of PA turned into everything from visiting the bank and arranging money to sorting out his love life and trying to take the tension out of his difficult relationship with his girlfriend, blonde divorcee and mother of two, Sheryl Kyle. It was like being a buffer (not that we didn't have our laughs, we did), but the presence of so many dominant figures in his life – like Sheryl in Rome and his adviser, Mel Stein in London, as well as his club, Lazio – soon caused him to be pulled in several directions, unsure of whom he should listen to.

I think there could be many reasons for writing this book, but perhaps my main motive is to allow a wider audience a glimpse of the real Paul Gascoigne behind the clown's mask. No other sports personality has been so loved and yet so criticized and misunderstood. Now you can know the truth and make up your own minds as to why Paul is unique.

All public figures have their private faces, and there are moments when even the greatest of them have their self-doubts. Paul Gascoigne is no different – he is just like the next man in the street, except for one small thing. He was born with a special talent and a great joy of life to go with it. He is the entertainer that we all need in our lives, the person who makes us feel a bit better about our daily humdrum existence.

As with most people in the limelight, Paul has an inner circle of advisers who are supposed to help him make the most of his talents on and off the pitch. Unfortunately, this doesn't always work in his favour and I intend to examine in detail the influences, positive and negative, of the various members of his entourage.

I hope in the following pages to strip away the gloss and let you have a closer look at a superstar and his friends and advisers, the high-pressured life of Italian football, and its affect on the friends and family of a world class footballer.

So who is Paul Gascoigne? Read on and find out.

THE START OF IT ALL

My first meaningful conversation with Paul Gascoigne occurred on 30 May 1990 at Lo Scoglie restaurant just outside Cagliari. It went like this:

Paul: 'Where do you come from?'
Me: 'Berkshire.'
Paul: 'Must be a lot of dogs there [cackle, cackle].'

It took me a few seconds to understand the accent, never mind the joke. I soon came to realize that kind of remark was typical of Paul Gascoigne, the cheeky, playful lad from Newcastle. He was the one who made the jokes and entertained the crowd. Even as an apprentice at Newcastle, he was like that. Sometimes it was mildly irritating, at other times over the top, but whatever the reaction it made you notice him – and in the competitive world of football that was vital.

A week before on 25 May, he had arrived with the England football team to compete in the 1990 World Cup Finals in Italy. It had been an arrival full of tension. Bobby Robson was under fire from his own national press over revelations that he was about to leave his job as England manager at the end of the World Cup, and also over his alleged colourful private life. The assault by the press on Bobby had been so intense that hardly anyone noticed Paul Gascoigne as he bounced down the steps of the Britannia Airways jet on that sunny morning in Cagliari. Not that people were unaware of him. It was difficult, in fact impossible, to ignore him. He was likeable, mischievous and a bit of a laugh; the group prankster and the fall guy for the jokes played on him by the rest of the team.

However, the young pretender nearly didn't make it at all into the Italian sunshine. England manager Bobby Robson had been undecided until the last minute whether to include Gascoigne in the World Cup squad. It wasn't until his brilliant performance against Czechoslovakia only a month prior to Italia '90 that his place had been secured.

'I didn't let the press know, but after the Czechoslovakia game, in my mind Gascoigne was part of the team,' says Bobby Robson. 'I thought he and Bryan Robson would make a very strong pair in midfield. Gascoigne had proved he could perform against top players. He had flair, imagination and spontaneity.'

That wasn't the only reason that Gazza nearly didn't make the party. On the eve of England's departure for Italy, he realized that he had left his passport at home, and friend Jimmy Gardner had to drive through the night from Gateshead to get it to him at the team hotel near Luton airport. Jimmy 'Five Bellies' was his best mate, having grown up with Gazza in Gateshead. When Gazza first played for Newcastle, Jimmy had often gone to training sessions and the players would take pot shots at him. He was an amicable lad and a tower of strength for Paul, especially during the World Cup days and later on in Rome.

The journalists, both British and Italian, were aware that Gazza was one of the emerging youngsters from an otherwise uninspiring pool of British talent. Giancarlo Galavotti, London based-correspondent of *La Gazzetta dello Sport*, had followed his career from 1987.

'Gascoigne was inconsistent, sometimes fantastic, sometimes mediocre. He wasn't mature and was rather a difficult character, but he was a British footballer who had a rare talent and skill on the ball.'

The British journalists were enthusiastic, although similarly cautious. Jeff Powell, one of the most experienced opinionists in the world of sport and chief feature writer for the *Daily Mail* says: 'He was very talented, but had a self-destruct element to him. England had not been producing really gifted footballers for some time and Gascoigne was an exception. He was the symbol of hope.'

As the symbol of hope boarded the Italia '90 team coach, he was unaware, as was everyone else, that in just six weeks time he would be a hero and have to cope with having the hopes and dreams of millions of people resting on his young shoulders. There had been quite a few promising upstarts before Gazza, kids who dreamt that they could be the next generation of footballing greats, but none had quite managed to capture the imagination of the hero-starved public. To satisfy the hopes of a nation, 'Gazzamania' was about to be born.

It didn't take Paul Gascoigne long to stand out from the crowd. Two days after the team's arrival, on 27 May, it was his twenty-third birthday and also the day of the official celebrations for the promotion of local team, Cagliari, to the prestigious Serie A. The local World Cup organizing committee had arranged for Bobby Robson to take a few of his players along to help Cagliari celebrate. Everyone was at the stadium, the local mayor and other dignitaries and, of course, our lovable Gazza, who couldn't resist playing up to the crowd. When the players went down to the pitch to meet the team before the match, Gazza amused himself and everyone else by plastering stickers on the backs of the local VIPs attending the match. Everyone thought this was quite a laugh; it was harmless and, more to the point, it relieved the heavy boredom of having to watch the game.

After the match, Bobby Robson and his players were taken by police escort back to their hotel. The atmosphere was incredible. Everyone was out on the streets celebrating, jumping up and down and hugging each other, dressed up in the team's colours with even their cars painted in blue and maroon. Perhaps this was the start of the affinity between Gazza and the Italians, for the way the Italians celebrate – loudly and with total gusto – is exactly in line with the Gascoigne character. It was certainly one hell of a way to celebrate a birthday.

That evening the England team had their own celebration for Gazza. Bobby Robson ordered a cake with a brush on top of it – referring to the time when the England manager described Gascoigne to a colleague on the bench as being 'daft as a brush', the player having disobeyed instructions during an important World Cup qualifying match. Various people gave speeches, including the birthday boy, who gave a brilliant send-up of himself, describing how he'd got so far in his career. It was Gazza at his best: amusing, quick thinking and entertaining.

'I was great at seven,' he started, 'at twenty I was the best player in the world, at twenty-one I was on seven grand a week...'

The audience loved it. Bobby Robson, in spite of his initial reservations, is a great Gazza fan and says about Gazza's presence in the World Cup: 'He was brilliant. Great for the group and great for the team. His bubbly personality could bring about a change in atmosphere and lift team spirits.'

Also part of the non-playing England contingent in Cagliari was another joker, violinist and football fanatic Nigel Kennedy and his girlfriend, Brix. Apart from a liking of the ridiculous, Nigel and Gazza have another thing in common – their outstanding talents. Nigel may clown around and seem to be an absolute twit, but get him on the subject of music and you will discover the serious and extremely well-informed side of Nigel Kennedy. He may appear not to give two hoots, but for between four and six hours every day in Sardinia he was in his hotel room practising. That is not the behaviour of a buffoon. It is almost the same with Gazza. Give him an impossible challenge and he will give you total dedication.

Only when things are easy, does he experience problems. Playing football comes so easily to him, that he has to have some other insurmountable challenge to conquer in order to keep him interested in life.

It is strange but both Nigel and Gazza need to be loved and accepted by the public, even if they try and pretend the opposite, but in their efforts to be liked they are often despised. It seems that genius is not always a kind companion.

Meanwhile, Bobby Robson had decided to bring the team out early for a week's holiday with their wives and girlfriends, so the players could relax before getting down to the business of match preparation. Several of the team had come on their own: Trevor Steven because his wife was about to have a baby; Chris Waddle because he arrived late, having been delayed by the end of the French season; and Gazza, well Gazza because, who knows? For some reason he had decided not to bring his then long-standing girlfriend Gail Pringle along on holiday. (As he said to anyone who enquired: 'I'm the boss'.) For Gazza football and women just did not mix. To a working-class lad from Newcastle who was used to drinking in the local working men's club in a room where women were banned, it was only natural to have a holiday with the lads, and not bring along the girlfriend. The only difference was that most of the lads had brought along their other halves.

Chris Waddle had the dubious honour of sharing a room with Gascoigne, an experience that very few people would have volunteered for, as Gazza was extremely hyperactive. Not only that, but he insisted sleeping with both the lights and television on. This fear of the dark seemed to stem from the horrific experience when he was a 12-year-old of seeing Steven Spraggon, the brother of his best friend Keith, run over by a car. Steven had been coming out of the local corner shop back home in Gateshead when, as he ran out into the road, a car had hit him and killed him. It was one of the most traumatic experiences of Paul's childhood, and had come soon after his father suffered a brain haemorrhage, from which it had taken John Gascoigne a while to recover. These incidents just added to Paul's insecurity and emotional fragility.

In Cagliari, however, the jokes were flying around as he offered Chris Waddle a coffee, and when his room-mate commented on its frothiness, Gazza explained to him it was cappuccino. It was, in fact, bath foam!

True to form, after a few days sunshine in Sardinia, the weather gradually got worse. Nothing, though, could distract Paul from his daily tennis matches with fellow tennis fanatics Trevor Steven, team co-ordinator Giacomo Malvermi and Steve Hodge. These were real battles of the titans, with the competitive spirit threatening to boil over on several occasions. On 29 May England played Cagliari in a warm-up friendly in the local town of Pula, winning 6–0. This was followed by a three-hour tennis match played by our champions and won 4–6, 6–3, 7–5 by Gascoigne and Hodge. At twenty-three the Newcastle youngster had boundless energy to go alongside his great natural talent. Together, these qualities would help see him to the top.

The holiday, however, was coming to an end. Soon, the serious business of competing in the World Cup would start. The England team flew to North Africa to play their final friendly against Tunisia, drawing 1–1 only after Wolves striker Steve Bull had saved some red faces by scoring a late equalizer. It did not take long for the press to go onto the attack, with headlines like 'World Chumps' appearing for all to read back home.

The very brief honeymoon period with the press, which occurred during the holiday week, was now over and the pressure was back on. Paul never had an easy relationship with the press, partly due to the fact that he had been slammed by the tabloids. He didn't seem to understand that he couldn't take the mickey out of journalists and expect not to read something detrimental in the papers the next day. The other reasons behind the press misunderstandings could be attributed to the advice regarding the media that was given by his advisers, who were not media experts. Money would be asked for any commercial venture, including interviews for the children's magazine *Shoot*. Mel Stein, who negotiated with the papers on Gazza's behalf, used to say, 'I educate my players that time is worth money, so they don't give "free" interviews.'

Gazza did not attend any press conferences for the duration of the World Cup and when the Italian press, who were desperate for information as they had three sports papers to fill, attempted to compromise by submitting written questions for him to answer, they were handed back one word replies. For example, 'Do you think England gave a good performance last night?' would be answered by 'Yes'. This does not endear the journalists to players, as they are in the main, with a few very obvious exceptions, professional people doing a job of informing the ticket-buying fans about their favourite teams. More footballers should realize that without journalists, fans wouldn't get so much information about their team, and no team information would mean no hype, no hype no money, and without money no huge salaries.

England were one of the seeded teams in Cagliari, much to the consternation of the Spaniards who felt they also merited seeded status in view of their World Cup pedigree. FIFA, taking into consideration the hooligan supporter element, decided to isolate England on the island of Sardinia. It was a move that worked very well. The Sardinians and the English are both island breeds and after a few minor run-ins, developed a healthy respect for each other.

It was with some trepidation that England approached the first match against old adversaries, the Republic of Ireland. For Bobby Robson, especially, it was vital the team played well. After all the flack from the press he wanted to prove that he could produce a side capable of winning the World Cup. At this point even he didn't know what an ace he had up his sleeve in the unpredictable but talented Gascoigne.

'He has everything that goes into making a great footballer,' former Newcastle team-mate Glenn Roeder once commented. 'His only achilles heel is pace, but apart from that he has perfect balance, vision, a football brain, awareness of what is going on around him, a fantastic first touch, dribbling skills, and shooting skills. He can score goals and is strong in attack when he puts his mind to it. Most footballers are lucky to have one or two of these assets.'

On 7 June, the day before the opening match of the 1990 World Cup finals, golf equipment manufacturer Wilson put on a golf tournament for the England team and other willing participants. Getting into the Gazza frame of mind, they even provided exploding golf balls, which emitted clouds of white dust when hit. Gazza was obviously quite pleased by all this, so after having a few good drives he climbed into his golf cart, hit the accelerator... and promptly ran into Bobby Robson! Fortunately, Bobby was not scarred mentally or physically by the incident and did not seem unduly surprised. The occasion did serve to relax the players and also relieve the tension as the countdown began towards the first match against the Irish.

The World Cup kicked off in Milan the next day, with Argentina playing the unfancied Cameroon. Cameroon surprised all the pundits by winning 1–0, and suddenly the world sat up and took notice. Maybe this wasn't going to be a predictable World Cup after all. Down in the England team hotel at Is Molas, everyone was delighted by the Cameroon victory, although they would be less delighted when they came up against the physical Africans in the quarter-finals in Naples, in a few week's time.

England met the Republic of Ireland on 11 June, and it was back to old predictability. Even the weather was out in sympathy, dark thunder clouds gathering threateningly just before the match. 'I'm glad we came out three weeks early to acclimatize,' Bobby Robson muttered as he led the England team out onto the pitch. The players had been in good humour as they travelled to the match, singing the team song

'World in Motion' and listening to Phil Collins.

In the team line-up before the match, Gascoigne stuck his tongue out during the national anthem, which was typical of him going over the top, and then found that things were harder than had been predicted. The match was as bad as the weather, a scrappy, uninspired battle of the long ball. Gascoigne's talents hardly got a look in as he tried to chase the ball round the pitch, and it finished 1-1 with Lineker opening the scoring and Sheedy replying for the Irish. Not an awe-inspiring start to England's group and the journalists were merciless in their collective condemnation of the performance. The players drowned their sorrows with the cans of beer placed on the team coach in spite of the alcohol ban imposed by the Italian authorities. Next time it just had to better, especially as England were to meet European Champions, Holland. The cynics were already predicting a swift exit for the bedraggled English, if they continued playing as badly as they had in the first match. But then things did change.

For most of the Irish game, Gascoigne had watched helplessly as the ball sailed over his head, bypassing the midfield. The old system of playing off set-piece corners and free kicks, as suggested by the FA coaches, had simply not suited his game. Now Bobby Robson decided to do things his way, and go back to what he knew best – instructing his team to keep the ball on the floor and adopt a more attractive passing style of football with the midfield heavily involved.

Before the game against the Dutch, there was a chance to relax. The day after the disastrous game against the Irish, several of the players including Gazza headed down to where the press were staying, at the Forte village complex, just down the road from the England team hotel. The village was full of peacocks and bicycles, the one not necessarily living in harmony with the other, as the peacocks found to their cost when confronted by Gazza in the saddle of his new toy, bearing down on them at full steam! Fortunately, there were no casualties on either side, and Gazza once again had defused a tense situation by bringing a bit of humour into the proceedings after the disappointment of the Irish match. It was to be a recurring theme that, in spite of his own state of mind, his sensitivity would ensure that he would always try to cheer up his team-mates and make sure everyone was happy.

The day after the fun and frolics in the Forte village, Nigel Kennedy entertained the players with his talented musicianship. But at the same time he was charming everyone with various renditions of both classical and pop music, another scandal was brewing – the four-in-a-bed hostess scandal. Late that night, I was confronted by John Jackson and Chris Boffey from the *Daily Mirror* and the *News of the World* respectively, who enquired as to whether there was any truth in the rumour that local hostess Isabella had been found in bed with *three* England players at the same time. It all seemed too ridiculous to consider and so it was dutifully denied and forgotten about until the next day, when headlines screamed from most of the British tabloids. Gazza's name was never mentioned, but like the others he found it all quite a laugh. The story ran for a few days and then eventually fizzled out; there had been very little else for the journalists to write about in the absence of the predicted riots on the terraces, so any newsworthy story was worth its weight in gold.

The team had by this time a chance to settle in and get to know the locals, and they soon won their respect and support. Many Italians had expected a pack of beer-swilling monsters (as had the organizers) and were pleasantly surprised when they encountered a disciplined outfit dedicated to the job in hand. England captain Bryan Robson's steady influence was important in keeping the younger players like Paul Gascoigne under control, as was the presence of other members of the old guard like Peter Beardsley, Peter Shilton and Gary Lineker. The general atmosphere at the team hotel was one of calm amidst the steady stream of jokes. Importantly for Gascoigne, he had the support and stability of his senior team-mates as well as many past heroes who were in Cagliari as part of the England team's extended family. The late Bobby Moore, with his quiet dignified manner gave the young Gascoigne a shining example of how he should conduct himself; Lawrie McMenemy, a fellow Geordie, was an important point of reference for Gazza; and the more extrovert Ron Atkinson, who was in Cagliari as a British TV commentator, provided some colour and hard won experience.

Gazza felt protected in this atmosphere so full of past and present footballing heroes, and was more than happy to play the clown with his team-mates but keep away from the press and out of the public eye. He didn't have to show he was brilliant anywhere except on the football pitch and this was important for his peace of mind and his development into one of the star players of the tournament.

In many ways the World Cup was ideal for Paul. Not only was he to a large degree protected from the press, he was in the sunshine with his friends, having a bit of a laugh and playing the game he loved. It was more like a footballing holiday. None of the foreign teams worried him in the slightest, simply because he had not come across them before. He understood the importance of matches against Liverpool and Manchester United, but when it came to playing international sides like Holland and Egypt, he had no idea of the players he would be facing. It was pointed out that when he played for Newcastle against Arsenal for the first time, the Newcastle manager was going on about Kenny Sansom – what a great defender he was and how they would have to be aware of his sniping runs from the back. After what seemed like a few minutes Gazza, looking bemused by it all, sighed and turned to a team-mate, asking, 'Who is this Kenny Sansom? Is he a good player?'

The fact that he had never heard of a player capped 80 times for England at full-back did not seem to bother Gazza. He had no respect for other players' reputations and he took them for what they were on the day. His attitude was that it was no good being petrified by Van Basten, until the Dutchman proved to you he was a great striker on the pitch. Everyone, after all, could have their off-days.

On 16 June the England team travelled to the Sant 'Elia stadium in Cagliari to meet Holland. According to football writer, Jeff Powell, it was '...a watershed match, and enabled England to surprise Holland and to take them on at football'. If there had not been any upheavals off the field, there was certainly about to be one on it.

On the team coach Gazza was on top form. He led the team in loud renditions of 'Let's all Shag a Hostess' and other philosophical ditties, as well as the now much loved 'World in Motion'. While Luciano Pavarotti was taking 'Nessun Dorma' to new heights on British television and the pop charts, 'World in Motion' was inspiring the England team to greater heights on the pitch.

As the match got underway it was obvious that Gazza was in his element and he soon showed the England fans his full repertoire of skills and tricks. Bobby Robson remembers his performance vividly.

'He was out there on the same pitch as world-class players like Marco Van Basten and Ruud Gullit, and he was as good as anyone on display on the day. He played as though he had been in the team for five years. He was confident and arrogant in the best possible professional sense. Finally, he could execute his skills without jumping ten feet into the air. He could play the one–two's that he was so good at. The kid was simply brilliant.'

With Mark Wright playing as a sweeper and with the two full-backs pushing up at every opportunity, England were able to bolster their midfield and create a platform for some incisive attacks. Gazza was a revelation, forever in the thick of the action. His international reputation had soared by the time he came off the pitch at the end of ninety minutes. The 0–0 draw belied a superb England performance. The match had been gripping, entertaining and skillful – it had been a long time since anyone had said that about an England match. There had also been moments of humour such as when Gazza, in a tussle for the ball with Van Basten, paused to quiz the Dutch striker on how much he earned. This would have been typical of Gascoigne and something he would have done with no malice but just out of curiosity, thinking it was nothing out of the ordinary. As far as the football was concerned, however, there had been a mini-revolution.

Both in training and on the pitch Paul Gascoigne was becoming more authoritative and more confident. Bobby Robson says that he developed a lot during the England training sessions.

'He became more responsible, he always listened and was receptive to instructions. He made you feel respected as a manager.'

Former team-mate and best friend Glenn Roeder sees another side to this 'receptiveness' and general impression of always listening to the manager.

'Managers and coaches would moan at him before the game and at half-time, about running with the ball. Rather than get into arguments with managers, he used to say, "Yes, boss, I'll lay it off" and so the boss would be pleased. Then as soon as the game started he'd do his own thing – but most of the time his own thing is so good that you can't moan at him.'

His debut match for the Newcastle first-team in the autumn of 1985 had been very much like that. In an away match against Southampton, the score was 0–0 with a few minutes to go. Glenn Roeder, takes up the commentary:

'Nearing the end of the match, Gascoigne picked up the ball fifteen yards outside his own box and facing his own goal. Most experienced players would have cleared it into the stands. Jimmy Case was marking him and we were all screaming at him to clear the ball but, no, he controlled it and started dribbling towards his own penalty box. Now the Southampton centre forward came at him, but you did not know where to go to get a pass from Gazza. If he did pass a short ball to you, you would just have to boot it down the middle and get it away, because you were eighteen yards from your own goal. He ended up in his own penalty box with Jimmy Case up his backside. Suddenly, he dropped his shoulder and went the opposite way, turned, and then dribbled the ball out of the penalty box to the half-way line. At seventeen, you just did not do those things unless you were Paul Gascoigne. It summed up what he was going to do with his career. It was the most brilliant debut performance I have ever seen.'

On 21 June 1990 England met Egypt for the final match in their group. All four teams had the same number of points, so the last match would decide who went on to the next round and who went home. At the same time that England were playing against Egypt, Holland and Ireland were battling it out in Palermo. Everyone expected Holland to beat Ireland, and England to edge past Egypt. In fact on a tense, hot night, Holland scored first in Palermo to lead the group, but in the second half The Irish, against all the odds, equalized. Then, Mark Wright headed in for England, which turned out to be the final goal of the night. So it ended with England on top of the group, with Holland and the Republic of Ireland tying for second place.

After his brilliant performance against Holland, Gazza did not play that well against Egypt. Players of the calibre and experience of former Tottenham and England striker Gary Lineker believe that it is easy to be consistent when you are a normal player, but when you can do special things, create things that other players cannot do, there will always be a level of inconsistency, as you cannot always perform at the same high level.

So England set off to meet the Belgians in Bologna, the Dutch travelled to Milan to meet the Germans, while the Irish came up against the Romanians in Genoa. One person who was missing on the flight from Cagliari to Bologna was Bryan Robson. Injury had finally overcome his heroic efforts and he had quietly travelled home, avoiding any fuss so as not to upset the team. His departure was a sad moment for the players. His partnership with Gazza had been vital for many reasons, not least on a psychological level. However, it was also the moment for Paul Gascoigne to take centre stage. This he did – in the most dramatic way possible.

The atmosphere was very tense in Bologna. The relationship between the team and the press had deteriorated to the point of mutual insults. There was no communication between the two parties, and when Paul Parker decided to try and improve relations by opening up more to the press, Gascoigne took matters into his own hands and threw a cup of water at him from the team coach. Not surprisingly, Gazza got a roasting in the papers the next day.

The team hotel was charged with a strange electricity. After a month in Cagliari, living in their own little world on the island, the England players were suddenly back in the cut and thrust of the World Cup. Some of the people who had been with the team in Cagliari travelled on to Bologna, but it didn't really help. The rhythm had been changed. In some ways it seemed as if the spell had been broken. Bobby Robson was seen sitting dejected in the hall of the hotel, his head between his hands. Undoubtedly, he missed the team leader and inspiration, Bryan Robson. 'Robbo' was not only the captain in the technical sense of the word, but also the person who kept the whole thing together. He sorted out arguments, made sure the new players were happy, and liaised with the manager, warning him of any discontent amongst the ranks. In Cagliari, I watched him several times when the team was together. In the dining room, for example, he used to work his way round the tables, having a quiet word with those youngsters he knew were nervous, or shooting a warning glance at those who were getting out of hand. He was Bobby's right-hand man, and you could see he was sorely missed, as

England struggled to come to terms with his departure both on and off the pitch.

The Novotel, just outside Bologna, was also a big change from the Is Molas hotel in Cagliari. There the players had been in cool, calm isolation with the beach a few minutes down the road, guards on the gate, and a golf course in the back garden. Suddenly they were back in the urban connurbations; it was like going to sleep in the wilds of the Yorkshire Moors and waking up in Coronation Street. In Cagliari they had the hotel to themselves, with occasional visits from VIPs like Sports Minister Colin Moynihan. Here, there were other guests and a not very isolated swimming pool, which was open to the general public at weekends. Bobby Robson watched disconsolately as the players ambled amongst the bronzed bodies and wandered round the concrete corridors of the modern building.

If Bobby Robson was gloomy on arrival, he was hopping mad on match day, when he glanced out of the window and saw Gazza smashing balls about the tennis court, just a few hours before England were due to meet Belgium. Playing tennis was just another way of easing the tension for Gazza. His brain, hands and nervous system were rather like a complicated electrical circuit, and there was a danger that the whole thing would overheat and blow a fuse. The trouble was, he had to be saved from himself on more than one occasion, and tiring himself out before such an important match was one of those times.

On the night of 26 June, England came up against Belgium in Bologna. It was always going to be a difficult match. Midfield star Enzo Scifo was on form and there were several other Belgian players who had impressed in the earlier games. The pressure was on England. They could not get knocked out now when the Irish were already through to the quarter-finals, having beaten Romania. The English fans had been on a rampage in Rimini and there had been mass arrests, much to the consternation of Colin Moynihan, who had worked day and night to ensure that the Italians had full support from the British government. Tempers were beginning to fray, and it needed a good performance by England in Bologna that night to calm the nerves.

After a neurotic first twenty minutes when the England team seemed to be oblivious to any game plan, they gradually took command of the match and began pushing forward, but it was a thankless task trying to break through the massed ranks of the Belgian defence and at full-time the score was still 0–0. As extra-time wore on, the players were beginning to tire, and it looked odds-on that the game would have to be decided on penalties. Then, with only minutes to go, England were awarded a free kick near the left touchline about 40 yards from the Belgian goal. Gascoigne stepped up to take it. 'Get it into the box!' yelled Bobby Robson. With consummate skill he did just that, the ball floating unerringly towards David Platt who, with his back to goal, freed himself from his markers, swivelled, and volleyed home a cracking goal. England were through to the quarter-finals and their fans were ecstatic. The one sour note to the proceedings had been the yellow card Gascoigne picked up during the game. It was an incident which was to have emotional consequences later on in the tournament.

The next day at the press conference, the media made peace with Bobby Robson and the players. It all looked like settling down once again.

Later that day the England party flew to Naples to prepare for their clash with Cameroon in the quarter-finals. If Bologna had been Coronation Street, Naples was Dante's *Inferno* – incredibly hot, noisy and chaotic. However, for the players it was back to the beach and a holiday atmosphere, with the team staying at Vetri sul Mare, a rather lovely seaside resort on the Amalfi coast. The press were based in other resorts stretching up and down the coast, while I was in the centre of Naples opposite the incredible Castello dell'Uovo, or 'Egg Castle', which had been turned into a press centre.

The Neopolitans are very good at improvising, and are also very hospitable. Whereas after the England–Belgium game, it had been difficult to get the post-match beer on to the England team coach following the ban on alcohol (which the Bolognese had decided, horror of horrors, should extend to the participating teams as well as the fans), in Naples things were much more flexible. All alcohol was forbidden with the exception of wine, which for the duration of the ban was considered non-alcoholic. This was mainly due to the fact that the match was on a Sunday, and the Neopolitans had no intention of having Sunday lunch without wine. So a compromise was reached, and it all worked very well. It was strange how so many people got tipsy on 'non-alcoholic' wine!

If the hotel in Cagliari had been the epitome of peace and tranquillity, and the Novotel in Bologna had a few tourists and inhabitants wandering about the place, then the place in Naples was non-stop action. Every day the ground-floor reception rooms were full of people getting married, christened or buried, or all three. The England team were allowed to have the first floor, but the ground floor was reserved for these celebrations. At least the players didn't get bored; all they had to do was sit in the reception area and watch life pass by. It was a welcome distraction for the irrepressible Gazza, as he could amuse himself and have a laugh without even having to leave the hotel.

To survive in Naples the best thing to do is to throw away your timetable, as time simply does not exist. This seemed to suit Gazza down to the ground. On the first day, Gascoigne, Waddle, Bull and McMahon decided to drive to the beach with my car and driver, apparently with the permission of Bobby Robson. Wandering about on a public beach in Naples was not necessarily the most advisable thing for four international footballers to be doing on their afternoon off, and it was not long before I started to worry. Perhaps the had been kidnapped by the Camorra (the Neopolitan mafia), or been assaulted by fans? Or had they got lost? It was over an hour before my driver returned. By now, my concern had reached fever pitch, so we rushed down to the beach in the hope of finding them. After a few minutes of searching under the deckchairs and amid the sandcastles, we came across the miscreants, sitting quite happily and taking in the scenery. Gascoigne was basking in the sunshine, as red as a beetroot, while Chris Waddle, his official 'minder' was trying to persuade him to cover up before he burnt to a cinder. The other two were in the shade sipping a cool drink.

Eventually, and only after some persuasion, Gazza got up and promptly strolled off to play on the pinball machine in a beach arcade. Word soon got round that a few of the England players were on the beach and some of the locals appeared. Gazza, however, soon had things under control and started to entertain his audience by playing card tricks. Everyone loved this – it was plain to see how comfortable Gazza was in a situation he always preferred compared to the razzmatazz that comes with being a superstar, such as media appearances and sponsorship deals.

Being in Naples was like being in the circus for Gazza, but as Bobby Robson said referring to his performance on the pitch: 'The biggest lesson Gascoigne had to learn was that you couldn't be part of the circus all the time.' In other words he couldn't have a piece of the action all the time, and had to learn when to push himself and when to hang back and let others sort things out.

The atmosphere had reverted once again to being relaxed and optimistic. The worries of Belgium had been left behind, Bobby Robson was on top form, and together with Glen Kirton, his head of external relations, and press man, David Bloomfield, he was looking forward to the quarter-final match. England had already progressed far beyond expectations, and in a World Cup that was bereft of an obviously outstanding team, they were in with a chance. The team had come a long way since their rather dismal arrival in Cagliari over a month before. Most of the players were in good form and several of them, especially Platt, Walker, Parker and Gascoigne, were attracting interest from a number of foreign clubs. Italy were expected to win the tournament and Germany were very strong contenders, but England had an outside chance. The most likely final was Italy against Germany, but the most romantic one would be Italy against England. Different styles, different pace, but similar heart.

On 30 June the Irish, despite performing bravely, went out of the World Cup, beaten 1–0 by Italy in the Olympic stadium. After the game, the camaraderie between the two sets of fans was in clear evidence, as they danced in the streets outside the ground. Meanwhile in Naples, Bobby Robson was dreaming of going one better and getting through to the semi-finals. It was the least he deserved, being a decent, hard-working man who merited better things than the dreadful treatment he got from certain quarters of the press. He believed he had the squad to realize his dream: Gary Lineker, in form and hungry for goals; a solid defence with a choice from Mark Wright, Terry Butcher, Paul Parker and Des Walker, with Peter Shilton as the rock-solid goalkeeper; the reliability of Peter Beardsley, David Platt and Stuart Pearce; the creativity of Chris Waddle and the injury-prone John Barnes; and the unpredictable yet undeniable genius of Paul Gascoigne. Their challenge was a World Cup quarter-final in the San Paolo stadium against the Cameroon, the surprise team of the tournament, who were short on tactics but heavy on raw talent and physical presence.

At the press conference the day before the match, Bobby Robson admitted he would be tying Gascoigne to a chair to allow the others to get some rest. Gazza was still very hyper-active but, harnessed in the right way,he became a positive part of the team's preparation.

England's quarter-final tie had attracted a large British contingent of supporters, among whom were two govern-ment ministers, Colin Moynihan, Minister of Sport and

Michael Howard, Minister of Employment. The latter, keen to exploit all good photo opportunities, insisted on having his picture taken with two ex-Youth Training Scheme boys, Platt and Gascoigne. Also in the VIP box was former US Secretary of State, Henry Kissinger, and the men who had made the World Cup happen, Antonio Matarrese and Luca di Montezemolo.

Down on the pitch the players had started to lose weight before our very eyes. It was stiflingly hot and very humid. At half-time things looked fairly good. Even though the team hadn't been as confident in defence as they might have been, England were 1–0 up thanks to a 26th-minute goal by David Platt. The situation changed rapidly in the second-half when the Cameroon were awarded a penalty from which Kunde scored, after a rash foul by Gazza on Milla. This was followed five minutes later in the 68th minute by another Cameroon goal. Suddenly the Africans were 2–1 up and England were looking very shaky indeed. Gascoigne was not much in evidence and the midfield seemed to be suffering from a lack of communication. If the Africans hadn't been so naive they would have kept things tight and gone on to win the match. Instead, they continued to press forward, leaving themselves exposed to Gary Lineker, the one England player who looked capable of turning the game. Late in the second half he was awarded a penalty which he coolly put in the back of the net, and then in extra-time he scored again. The final result was 3–2 to England. Thank God for Gary Lineker! Without his tactical brilliance and skill, England's dream would have been over.

Nevertheless, the improbable had happened and England were through to the World Cup semi-finals. It was the first time ever on foreign soil and the atmosphere in the press conference was euphoric. Whatever happened next, they would go out in style.

England arrived in Turin as the underdogs. Everyone expected Germany to win as on paper they were the stronger side. After Naples, Turin seemed almost like Switzerland, well organized with everyone aware of their various duties. This was the kingdom of the mighty Juventus and anyone who entered had to be aware of this. Getting into the last four meant that the eyes of the world were upon England. Dozens of journalists descended on the England team hotel and found the players, with the exception of a few including Gazza, happy to talk to them.

On the night of the match, the Stadi delle Alpi was packed to capacity. It was a sweltering night, not as humid as in Naples, but still hot and energy-sapping. The last two England matches had both gone to extra-time and the combination of heat and tiredness would become an important factor the longer the match went on. As the teams were getting prepared for the game in their dressing rooms, the mighty Gianni Agnelli decided to pay a visit to wish both England and Germany good luck. Agnelli was the Italian equivalent of the Queen, he was used to people bowing and scraping in his regal presence. As the Chairman of car giants, Fiat, and as someone who came from a Torinese noble family, he commanded the ears of all the major politicians, both at home and abroad. He counted men like the Aga Khan and Henry Kissinger as personal friends. However, Gazza was not aware of this and when Agnelli entered the England dressing room, Gazza thought he was probably just an old fan popping in to say hello, so he raised his thumb, grinned and said, 'Alright, mate.' Agnelli was captivated. Unused to being accepted just as a fan, he immediately took to Gazza, and has remained fascinated by him ever since. He often asks David Platt what Gazza is like, as though fascinated by the antics of a naughty child.

As the kick-off drew nearer, Bobby Robson took Gascoigne aside to give him a little lecture about Lothar Matthaus, and how to handle the German star.

'Listen to me, son, you're going to play against Matthaus. If you get out of position, or get undisciplined, Matthaus will come through our midfield like a tank and stick two goals past us before we can get our breath, and it will be your fault.'

'Boss, smoke your cigars and leave him to me.'

As soon as the match started, it was apparent that it was going to be a thriller. England had risen to the occasion in every way, and were proving to be hard opponents.

'This was Gascoigne's best match,' commented Jeff Powell. 'Psychologically the Germans were prepared to let England come at them in the first half. They were expecting a bit of a cavalry charge and then for us to tire. Well, they reckoned without Gary Lineker and, of course, without Gascoigne.'

The experience of the World Cup had produced a well balanced and exciting team. As expected, the English were pushing forward and looking for an opening to score; the Germans were responding but allowing the English to do most of the running with the hope they would tire themselves out and then let the Germans move in and run all over them. Unexpectedly, it was the Germans who went ahead first through an Andreas Brehme free-kick which was deflected into his own goal by Paul Parker. Twenty-one minutes later, Gary Lineker once again retrieved the situation for his team and equalized. England were thrown a lifeline. At home, 30 million people were glued to their television sets, waiting for a miracle to happen. As England poured forward, Chris Waddle hit the crossbar in the dying minutes of extra-time – but the winner refused to come for Bobby Robson's team. Henry Kissinger was in the crowd that night and commented, 'It is the best match of the tournament. Whoever wins this will win the World Cup.' Prophetic words indeed.

Under the floodlights, Gazza was having the game of his life. He was everywhere in midfield, controlling the ball, looking up and picking out his team-mates with pinpoint passes. But then tragedy struck when Jose Wright, the Brazilian referee booked the England player for a foul on the German full-back, Thomas Berthold. Gazza went to pieces. Realizing that he would miss the final if England went through, and having put everything he had into this match, his confidence went in a matter of seconds and he started crying the famous tears. The booking was much criticized at the time, and it wasn't until I met up with Wright a few years later, that I discovered the truth of the matter. The booking had not been just for the tackle, but for his cheek during the whole match. According to Wright, Gazza had already overstepped the mark a few times, and the tackle was the final straw that broke the camel's back.

Gary Lineker was indicating frantically to the bench that Gascoigne had 'gone', but there was very little Bobby Robson could do at this stage. They just had to 'hang on in there' and make the most of the situation.

At the end of extra-time, the score was still 1–1. It was down to penalties with Gascoigne as one of the nominated penalty-takers. However, he was clearly in no state of mind to take one. As it turned out, he did not have to. In fact, it was one of the most important lessons that he learnt from the World Cup – that to be a great champion, you have to have nerve as well as talent.

On the night of the semi-final, he had been a constant source of inspiration for his team, even if he did lose his bottle after the booking. Lineker, Platt, Beardsley, Pearce and Waddle lined up to take the penalties for England. The first three scored, the last two missed, and Germany were through to the final. Six weeks had been condensed into a few minutes of pain and excitement. Then it was all over, except for the match in Bari to decide who would take third place.

There followed emotional scenes in the dressing room. Gascoigne was hugging his team-mates and crying, and most of the players were totally deflated. They had come so close.

'For a while, I really thought we would go right through to the final. We could have won it, I know we could,' said Bobby Robson.

I agreed with him, England were hot and on form, and if they had got past the Germans, I would have put money on them lifting the Cup. As it was England won the fair play trophy, which was collected on the night of the final by Bobby and the prolific Gary Lineker. It was a fitting tribute to Bobby, a fair man who had never lost his professionalism or his temper, even when under the kind of pressure that would make most men crack up.

Meanwhile, the star of the show did not know it yet, but after that night in Turin, life would never be the same for him. Paul Gascoigne was about to find out that his tears of frustration were to make him the people's hero.

SUPERSTARDOM

The England team returned from Italy to a hero's welcome, with thousands of people waiting to greet them at Luton Airport. Most of the attention, of course, was focussed on Paul Gascoigne, as the coach carrying the players did a tour of celebration around the streets of Luton.

England's World Cup star managed to escape for a few days back to Gateshead, by hiding in the back of his father's van to avoid the crowds. Once on familiar territory, Gazza felt protected again. The familiar surroundings of home and places like the Dunston Working Men's Club always had a calming effect on him, as he knew he would be treated like anyone else. Not that the locals weren't proud of him, but they showed it in their own low-key way, and that helped him to keep his feet on the ground.

Gazza is very influenced by the people surrounding him. His own inner insecurity has always sought approval from external influences he considers worthy of attention. In Newcastle, he had his family, who were very important to him, plus then girlfriend Gail, and Glenn Roeder and his family. It was Glenn's influence that was so important in the development of his football talent, and it was the stabilizing effect of Glenn's wife, Faith and their two children Holly and William, that helped keep Gazza in check while he was in London.

After the excitement of the World Cup, Gazza decided to take a rest and go on holiday with Gail. She had been his childhood sweetheart; they had met when Gazza played in her father's Sunday team and she had stood on the touchline to watch. Gail was quite reserved, which suited Gazza's more extrovert character; she was also a local northern girl and very much part of the same cultural upbringing. When Gazza moved to London, she went too, but she found it hard to fit in and hated life in the big city.

The holiday turned out to be a disaster, with Gazza constantly harassed by autograph hunters. This also led to problems in his relationship with Gail, so much so that the two of them decided on their return to split up and go their separate ways.

Meanwhile, the Italians were showing the first signs of interest in Gascoigne's outstanding talent. Immediately after the World Cup, the director of the organizing committee, Luca di Montezemolo – who was very close to Juventus owner Gianni Agnelli, and soon to be appointed executive vice president of the club – invited Jeff Powell and I to lunch at his luxurious apartment in the heart of Parioli in Rome. Being one of Montezemolo's press consultants, I was well acquainted with him. As we sat round the stylish table enjoying a lunch of risotto and salad, the conversation turned to the England team.

Having grown up alongside men like the late Bobby Moore and Terry Venables, Jeff Powell was considered to be an expert on the game and someone who was well tuned-in to developments in international football. Montezemolo asked Jeff's opinion about three players, David Platt, Des Walker and Paul Gascoigne. Jeff was honest in his views, he felt David Platt even though not such an outstanding talent as Gascoigne, had the right character to fit into Italian football. He was not only a worker, but he had a very highly tuned sense of public relations and business interests. He worked hard at projecting the right image and would be an asset for any club.

Des was one of the best defenders to come out of the World Cup, and although the Italians don't usually purchase defenders, having a large pool of their own, it really wouldn't cost them any more to bring Des to Italy than to buy an Italian player. Besides, they would be getting a player with international experience. As far as Gascoigne was concerned, the appraisal was a little more difficult. Although undoubtedly an outstanding natural talent – and everyone had seen that he was capable of great things on the world stage – there was the question of his character and temperament.

The Italian football league, Serie A, is considered by most experts to be the best of its kind in the world. The rewards that come from playing with the best players in the world are great, but the pressures are sometimes almost unbearable. Paul Gascoigne had lost his composure during the semi-final with Germany, when the pressure had been great, but not as intense as he would find in Italy. Also, one had to take into consideration Ian Rush's difficulties at Juventus. This had had nothing to do with Montezemolo, who is a brilliant strategist and manager. Most of the fault for the Welshman's failure rested with his club Juventus. That saga instilled a note of caution into any chairmen's minds when it came to dealing with foreign players, especially with the three Englishmen now arousing the interest of Italian clubs.

In the meantime, back in England, Gazzamania was taking hold of the country. The requests for the new England star to endorse products and take part in commercial activities were unprecedented for a footballer, and his two business advisers, Mel Stein and Len Lazarus, had to put their normal businesses on hold for six weeks while they sorted out Gazza's affairs. All sorts of things started to appear, from the more obvious Gazza balls and Gazza shin pads to the more bizarre products like toothpaste! It was almost as if he had achieved pop star status. People seemed to be attracted to his talent and also found his patriotism touching. It has to be remembered that over 30 million people tuned into the World Cup semi-final and saw Gazza shedding tears of frustration and disappointment as he realized his dream was over. It had touched the heart of the country and now everyone wanted to be part of it. He even had a much publicized meeting with the then Prime Minister, Margaret Thatcher, during which he dared to put his arm round the Iron Lady. Andy Roxburgh, Scotland team manager, who had also been present, gently reprimanded him for taking liberties, but Gazza just laughed it off and said he hadn't fancied the security man standing beside her – that man being Dennis Thatcher!

What effect was this adulation having on Paul Gascoigne? After all, he wasn't a pop star but a footballer and as one of his friends points out: 'He is happiest when he's playing football, either in training or in matches. If he could he would train morning and afternoon.' But outside influences were beginning to take over. He was being dragged around the country to attend functions, something he hates doing, and it wasn't long before his football started to suffer.

Gascoigne's manager at Tottenham, Terry Venables, had to take things in hand and ring Mel Stein, to tell him to go easy on his off-pitch activities, or ask him not to book anything for Paul after, say, the Wednesday before a match. Terry was in many ways Paul's saving grace. An intelligent and worldly man, he knew all about pressure as he had been a top-class footballer and then gone into that fish bowl existence of being a manager, not only in England but also for Barcelona in the Spanish league, which is not so very different to Italy in terms of media pressure and hysteria from the fans. He became a father figure to Paul and took the pressure off his private life. If Paul had a problem, like the water not working in his bathroom, he would go to Terry who would speak to Mel, to get it fixed. Terry knew that it was useless to tell Gazza to lock himself in his house in Hoddesdon and not go out, as he was under so much pressure to satisfy the demands of his admirers. So he took the sensible way out and provided him with encouragement on the pitch and a shoulder to cry on off it.

'I used to talk to him about things on a friendly basis, to let him know that I was thinking of him. He is the type of guy who needs to know that you are concerned about him. He needs more than someone who thinks only of him in footballing terms. You have to be in tune with him and find out the root of his problem. He may have come to me with a sore thumb and have asked, "Why am I feeling bad?" and the real reason wouldn't necessarily be the sore thumb. I always tried to get beyond the superficial problems and make him feel he had someone who cared for him.'

The responsibility for handling Gazza's business affairs belonged to his advisers, Mel Stein and Len Lazarus. Mel Stein had the higher profile of the duo; he negotiated the contracts and maintained day-to-day contact with Gazza's clients. A partner with London solicitors, Finers, he was developing the sports side of the business and specialized in representing footballers and other sports stars. 'I'm not an agent,' he was quick to tell me. 'I don't take a percentage, but I only work on a fee basis.' Many people, including Terry Venables, believe players are better off paying percentages to their representatives as they know exactly how much money they've got left. If an agent earns £1 million for his client and takes 10%, the player knows he has £900,000 left. If he pulls an hourly rate, he doesn't always know when the clock starts or when it finishes. Mel had been representing Gazza since just before the player's move from Newcastle to Tottenham.

As an accountant, Len Lazarus was responsible for investments and looking after Gazza's money. He was a co-signatory on many accounts and advised Gazza's as far as his financial were concerned. Glenn Roeder remembers on one occasion going with Gazza to the cashpoint to withdraw some money. When Glenn noticed that the account was substantially in the red and queried this, Gazza's reply was simple.

'Oh that, Len tops it up at the end of the month.'

During the 1988/89 season, Gazza admitted he hadn't seen his bank statement for seven months, but that he had 'people he trusted' looking after his money.

Together, Stein and Lazarus were making their client very rich, which in business terms was what they thought they had to do. It was, however, a very tricky situation. On the one hand, it was silly not to make as much money as possible while one could; on the other hand, here was a rather fragile and sensitive lad, who didn't like too much publicity. Stein and Lazarus had taken over his off-pitch life and their advice to him was to make money while he could, bearing in mind a football player's relatively short career.

One of the more controversial stunts was the recording of the Gazza LP, with hits 'Fog on the Tyne', an old Lindisfarne record that went to number one in the charts, and 'Geordie Boys', written by Mel Stein. Gazza suffered hell in the dressing room, and although he used to give as good as he got, it was yet more pressure and it was all getting rather wearing for him.

Back on the pitch, Tottenham's first match of the season was a home, against Manchester City. I went to the match with Michelle Lineker whom I had met during the World Cup when she had been watching her husband play for England. If Gazza was disorganized and chaotic in his private life, then Gary Lineker was the opposite. In Michelle, he had the ideal wife, totally supportive and understanding of her husband's job. Bright and personable, she ran Gary's life off the pitch with an efficiency that would have made most top PAs green with jealousy. Most importantly, she knew how to stay in the shadows without appearing to be a wallflower. Too many women want to be in the forefront and to be in the limelight, which means that eventually their relationship with their partners becomes a tug of egos and leads to bitter accusations and arguments. This was something that Gazza would have to deal with.

As the Tottenham players spilled out onto the pitch, both Gary and Gazza were given a hero's welcome by the fans, and in reply they turned in good performances. Gazza showed his old style with unselfish teamwork and at the same time several outstanding one-twos. It was an individual performance of excellence, unparalleled by anyone else in the British game. The match ended in a 3–1 win for Tottenham, with a goal from Gazza, and the fans went home in good heart, looking forward to more brilliance from their midfield genius. The following week, however, Gazza was substituted after a disappointing performance in the derby match between Arsenal and Spurs. When Derby paid a visit to White Hart Lane, he came back to form and scored, beating England goalkeeper, Peter Shilton, but he saved his best performance for the match against Newcastle the following Saturday, not only scoring but showing the brilliant command of midfield that had been so evident in the World Cup. As Terry Venables says, 'He came back from The World Cup at a new level, he went up to new heights in terms of brilliance and confidence. It wasn't only his individual skills that had improved, but also his team work. For a midfield player to score nearly 20 goals is almost unheard of.' By the time of the Spurs versus Crystal Palace match on 22 September 1990, Gazza had already scored five goals. He was looking good to reach the target of 20 that he set himself for that season after a bet with Glenn Roeder.

He was also having a great run in the Rumbelows Cup having scored four goals against Hartlepool in Spurs' 5–0 win, another against Bradford in the third round, and yet another against Sheffield United in the fourth. His league goal tally had reached twelve by the time Chelsea played Spurs on the 1 December, and his class was once more in evidence following the neat one–two combination through the Manchester City defence on 15 December, although City won 2–1. Paul Stewart and Gazza were proving to be an effective pairing in midfield and in the match against Luton on 22 December, which Spurs won 2–1, both players shone. They were good mates off the pitch and often went drinking together. Stewart was eventually sold to Liverpool and whether or not manager Terry Venables was sorry to see him go the Spurs manager made the best out of the situation by making a healthy £800,000 profit for Tottenham. Paul Stewart was bought for £1.5 million and sold for £2.3 million.

Gazza, though, seemed to be able to have it all, with his private life almost as colourful as his footballing abilities. There were a few games in which he didn't feature heavily, but for many he was the life force of the team. He was even enjoying the bright lights of London. With the fun, however, came the booze. Contrary to what many people believed, it had not started when he was at Newcastle.

'All this talk of Gazza being a heavy drinker when he was at Newcastle is rubbish,' Glenn Roeder points out. 'There was a great atmosphere among the youth team when Gazza was a part of it. The lads would train in the morning, then go down to the snooker hall and play all afternoon. This was often followed by a Chinese before going back home. The only time they had a drink was on a Saturday night in one of the clubs, and then after three shandies they were all on their backs.'

Whereas Gazza's life in Newcastle as a professional footballer possessed a charming innocence about it, in London it was different. He was now with people who didn't want to spend all afternoon in the snooker hall, and who didn't fall on their backs after three shandies. He started to change. External influences began to affect him in a negative way. The drinking problem had become more acute after the World Cup, when in an effort to blank out the constant attention he was getting from all walks of life, Gazza would drown his sorrows in the pub. Sometimes, this would get out of control. It was only his age and his incredible physical powers of recuperation that prevented his professional life from suffering too much.

His love life was also rather topsy turvy. With his new found superstar status, and having broken up with girlfriend Gail, he now had the choice of the pack, and he was making the most of it. Luckily, one of the big plus factors in his life was the fact that he had the stability of friends like the Roeders on hand to try and steady things down. Gazza was always popping in to see Glenn and Faith Roeder, sometimes on his own and other times with one of his many new 'girlfriends'. Glenn and Faith provided more than friendship for Paul, they were like an extended family. Glenn is ten years older than Paul and has always treated him rather like the younger brother that he never had, encouraging and guiding him in his career as a footballer, while his wife Faith was always prepared to be totally honest with Gazza, and bring him down to earth if necessary, especially regarding his choice of women. As someone put it, 'If he hadn't been a footballer, he could have allowed himself the luxury of the life style he had, but he was an athlete and sometimes the wild social life caught up with him.'

So girls came and went with frightening speed. Some stayed a night, some two but none lasted, and none seemed willing to try and stay the course – until blonde divorcee and mother of two, Sheryl Kyle, appeared on the scene. Gascoigne met Sheryl in a wine bar just before Christmas 1990, when she was on the point of breaking up from her husband, estate agent Colin Kyle. She lived near Paul in a large five-bedroomed house that was about to come under the threat of repossession as husband Colin's business suffered from the effects of the recession. Sheryl was one of the few girlfriends in Gazza's life to persevere with her man. Gazza would get home, switch on his answerphone and there would be several messages from Sheryl, asking him to call her and 'other things that you couldn't repeat'.

Not that this would be an easy undertaking. Paul was a typical Gemini – changeable, irrational, unpredictable and with a touch of duplicity to his nature, which sometimes made him take the easy way out of situations, leaving someone else to take the responsibility. Sheryl, as well as being stunningly attractive with a model's figure, was a very strong, dominant character, and in many ways just the type of woman Gazza needed. The fact that she had two children, five-year-old

Bianca and two-year-old Mason, didn't affect her relationship with Paul for a couple of reasons. First, in the beginning it wasn't a serious affair, just a fairly casual fling, although as time progressed the mothering qualities that Sheryl brought to the relationship clearly led Paul into a deeper involvement with her. Second, she used to offload the children onto ex-husband, Colin. As Colin says, 'I had the kids every weekend when we first broke up. They used to come on Saturday evening, and stay through to Monday.' Eventually daughter Bianca went to live with her Dad for three months, but the visits from Mason got less frequent and then stopped.

As far as Paul was concerned, Sheryl's children posed no problems. In many ways they actually helped the relationship, with Paul developing a natural affinity with them. In fact, from the children's point of view, she couldn't have picked a better stepfather. The child within Paul was instinctively reaching out, understanding and enjoying kids. Sometimes he gave the impression of liking children more than adults. After all, they accepted him for what he was. He would do anything for a child in trouble and was often reduced to tears on a children's ward or at seeing a child in distress. Paul even had his own foundation which helped teenage cancer patients and children with asthma problems. This was the more serious side of Paul Gascoigne that the press has often overlooked.

One chatty worker from the Make-A-Wish Foundation recalls, 'I was with a four-year-old girl who was waiting to meet Rod Stewart backstage after one of his concerts. She was pretty ill with leukaemia and some of the Spurs players were also around, most of them being slightly the worse for wear. Someone must have told Paul why the little girl was there, because he sobered up in a flash and came over and started chatting and entertaining her. He was absolutely wonderful and it made her evening.'

Not surprisingly, the public voted him BBC Sports Personality of the Year on 12 December 1990. It had indeed been an incredible year. In January, he had been just another footballer with Tottenham Hotspur, without a regular place in the England team. By July, all that had changed. He had become an international star, and financially his life had been transformed. Yet it had all happened so quickly that at times he felt almost overcome by all the attention. The only place to which he could escape was on the pitch, doing the only thing that really meant anything to him.

After the euphoria of the World Cup, Bobby Robson bowed out as national teal manager, having had enough of the pressures associated with the job, and went to Holland to manage PSV Eindhoven. In his place came Graham Taylor, ex-Aston Villa and Watford, the man who had established his credentials through his diplomatic handling of ebullient Aston Villa chairman Doug Ellis, and had led tiny Watford from the Fourth to the First Division. As he began the campaign to qualify for the 1992 European Championships in Sweden, Taylor realized he would have a tough task ahead of him. He was taking on a team that had far exceeded expectations by reaching the World Cup semi-finals in Italy, and now the fans were expecting nothing short of victory.

He came into the job with a burning desire to shake things up at the English FA, and try to drag it into the twentieth century. The problem with the FA is that whilst the world of football has moved into ever-increasing circles of sophistication, as far as commerce and sponsorship is concerned, it has remained a collection of rather loveable, football-mad fossils. Graham Taylor appreciated the importance of PR and saw the opportunities of steering the FA into the future, but it has been and still is, 'an uphill struggle'. Graham is a very steady bloke who doesn't allow things to get him down. He is also very determined and clear headed when it comes to realising his objectives. He knew he had to get the best out of Gascoigne if his team was to go all the way to the World Cup Finals in the States in 1994.

Graham chose Lawrie McMenemy as his right-hand man,

and he was to play a vital role in controlling the unpredictable Gazza. A reliable person who had great experience of handling temperamental footballers, Lawrie also had the additional advantage of coming from Tyneside. As far as the England set-up was concerned, both Taylor and McMenemy took over Terry Venables' job in being a surrogate father to Gascoigne, and this was to be an important factor when Gazza went to play in Italy.

One of the first decisions made by Graham Taylor caused an uproar in the media. It was the decision to drop Gascoigne from the team to face the Republic of Ireland in November 1990. The official reason given was that he didn't feel Gascoigne was suited to the Irish game, but the real reason was more complex. After a few months of Gazzamania and at the height of intense off-the-field pressure, Gascoigne was in no state to go out on the pitch and play. Graham took one look at him and realized that he just couldn't manage it. His eyes were darting about nervously and he was incapable of stringing a sentence together or concentrating on what was being said to him. In Graham's opinion, he was simply unable to last ninety minutes.

Graham knew that his decision would be immensely unpopular and cause him a lot of problems, but he felt he had to protect Gascoigne. So he stuck by his decision to drop England's World Cup hero. It wouldn't be the last time that he would have to keep his mouth shut to protect his brilliant but unpredictable star player. Eventually, the strain would take its toll and he would be forced to hint at the truth.

So the year 1990 drew to a close. For Paul Gascoigne, it had been a year of triumph in the World Cup followed by coming to terms with being a superstar. There were still a great many challenges lying ahead.

January 1991 started badly as Gazza got sent off in the game against Manchester United on New Year's Day. Off the field, rumours had begun to circulate about Tottenham's financial problems and the possibility of a management takeover. Terry Venables wanted to take control of the club and seemed the ideal person to do it in view of his popularity with the fans. The problem was getting the club's finances in order. By March, the story was gathering momentum, as was the news that an Italian club was interested in Gazza. While David Platt, a future Juventus recruit, was scoring a hat-trick in the Aston Villa versus Spurs match, Gazza was suffering from a hernia problem and struggling for full fitness. The pain and discomfort got so bad that it was finally decided to go ahead with an operation at the end of March, and Gazza was expected to be doubtful for the forthcoming FA Cup semi-final.

In the meantime, I had taken a trip over to the American Soccer Coaches Convention in Atlanta. In the States, soccer is immensely popular in the colleges, and various international coaches had gathered to offer advice and experience to the Americans. Graham Taylor and Andy Roxburgh were among the guest speakers. After the speeches, I sat down with Peter Stewart, of *Shoot* and *World Soccer* fame, to discuss with Graham Taylor what his plans were for the future. At that point, Graham was full of enthusiasm and ideas. He admitted to missing the buzz of being a club manager and having weekly or twice-weekly matches to prepare for, and he had found that the position of England manager was a very solitary one. Managers you thought were your friends suddenly became your enemies when the time arrived to prise a player away from his club for an international meeting. It was lonely at the top, as Graham was to find more and more to his cost. However, he was excited about the prospects of the European Championships in Sweden, and also by the wealth of talent he had at his disposal – players like Lineker, Gascoigne and Platt. He was happy to be in the hot seat and be the guiding hand behind the England team's fortunes.

I was in Italy at the end of February when I received a call from my friend Toni Damascelli, who informed me that football agent Dennis Roach was trying to sell Gascoigne in Italy on behalf of Tottenham. I rang Mel Stein, who expressed surprise as he knew nothing about any possible transfer deal, or even that Tottenham were considering selling one of their prime assets. In fact, Spurs had always insisted that they would not approve of any move to sell Gascoigne. However, a very different picture was emerging.

It appears that Tottenham were being put under pressure to take measures to put a halt to the huge debt that was building up with the Midland bank. Represented by Nat Solomon, the Midland – who would eventually take over proceedings at Tottenham – had already identified the club's greatest assets as Gary Lineker and Paul Gascoigne. Selling these two players would be number one on the priority list. So the club had enlisted Dennis Roach to test the water.

'My brief was to go and find out what the best price would be for Gazza in the current market conditions,' said Roach.

He discovered two clubs prepared to talk business. AC Milan made a half-hearted offer for the English star, but it was a more serious £5 million bid by Lazio that made Tottenham sit up and take notice. A series of highly secretive meetings was hastily arranged in London, one of the first taking place at the White House hotel in Regent's Park. It appears that Lazio's original offer of £5 million had not impressed Spurs, whose asking price for their star player was a cool £10 million.

By the time I met up with Mel Stein to discuss the situation, Lazio had already concluded a couple of meetings and felt they were going nowhere. At the beginning of March, Mel Stein and Len Lazarus became involved in what was already a difficult situation.

Mel Stein had been representing Gazza since just before his move from Newcastle to Tottenham in the summer of 1988. Prior to that time, Gazza's agent had been Alistair Garvie, a former assistant secretary of Newcastle Football Club. He had met Mel through attending various Newcastle away matches in London, having provided him with tickets for the game. What started out as a series of informal chats between the two about football soon developed into a friendship. Alistair left his safe job at Newcastle when he realized that there was a need for an experienced football person to act as the players' representative. He quickly signed up Chris Waddle and Gazza, and looked set for a lucrative career. Unfortunately, Alistair had one failing. He was a truly nice man, who would not have harmed a fly, and this led to him losing first Chris Waddle and then Paul Gascoigne to Mel Stein.

Three years on and Stein was riding on the crest of a wave, having developed a reputation as one of the top solicitors dealing with sporting superstars. However, some of my friends and colleagues expressed their doubts about him, and had warned me early on to be careful in my dealings with him. He was considered to be a very hard negotiator, and by being intransigent in certain deals, he had upset a few people, even though he was known for getting the best for his clients. At my first meeting with Mel, he had come across as a friendly, open, yet at the same time a rather contradictory character. He is a very instinctive person who makes his own decisions on how he feels about people. He also takes his Jewish religion very seriously. There were times during meetings with him when he would suddenly jump to his feet, put on his little round cap and start saying afternoon prayers, which according to the rules have to be said before sundown. He would follow the Jewish diet to the letter, and profess his love for fellow human beings. He even cultivated a certain eccentricity, such as wearing cartoon animal socks, and had a funny sense of humour, constantly taking the mickey out of people. Yet, at other times, Mel was quick to display a more analytical streak in his business dealings.

Len Lazarus, was a rather different sort of person. A partner with the firm of accountants Arram, Berlyn and Gardner, Len was very much the more level-headed of the two, plodding through life on an even keel, and not allowing his work with superstars to turn his head. I felt that Mel was very much more affected by the presence of stars. He loved the glitter and the glamour, and enjoyed taking centre stage. However, once you were accepted by Mel, he took you into the family circle and you became one of his people.

So together, Stein and Lazarus had taken over the day-to-day handling of Gazza's business affairs. This came at a price to Gazza: Stein's fees were £250 and Lazarus £130 per hour, which meant that with air fares and other expenses it would cost the player nearly £5,000 a day to have them in Rome for the day.

We flew to Milan for the European Cup tie between AC Milan and Marseille and discussed the possibilities of commercializing Gazza in Italy. As the country was such a lucrative market, I felt that there would be good opportunities to obtain publicity and advertising deals, especially bearing in mind Gazza's exceptional performance at the World Cup. If he ended up playing in Italy, the prospects would be even better. Following the meeting, we returned to the city to the impressive San Siro stadium, where we witnessed a 1–1 draw between Marseille and AC Milan – a good result for the French side.

The next day we flew down to Rome, and the sunshine. We were to meet the Italians at lunch in via Chiana. When we got there we were taken into a private section of the restaurant where Lazio chairman, Gianmarco Calleri was waiting for us with general manager, Carlo Regalia, and team manager, Maurizio Manzini. The lunch was very cordial and low-key. Lazio made it clear that they were serious in their intentions to buy Gascoigne, but they didn't know who they should be dealing with. They produced a letter signed by the Tottenham Chairman, which stated that Dennis Roach was the official Tottenham representative, able to discuss any interest in Gascoigne. Nothing definite was decided at that lunch, except to continue negotiations and see if the two sides could come to some form of agreement.

It seemed that Lazio wanted Gazza at any cost, and were prepared to accommodate any requests he made to help him settle in Rome. One of the things discussed at a later date was the suggestion by Mel Stein of the possibility of Glenn Roeder and family coming to live in Rome with Gazza, to supply a stable base for him. It would also be an opportunity for Glenn to assist in the coaching of the Lazio team. After a successful career with QPR, Newcastle and Watford, he was due to retire shortly and was ready for new challenges.

It was a wise decision to bring someone as level-headed as Glenn into the picture, as life in the world of Italian football has not proved easy for foreign players The rewards are great, especially the financial ones. Diego Maradona earned almost £1.5 million net a year with Napoli, and Marco Van Basten is on about the same with AC Milan. But the pressures are immense. The Italian media are infinitely more problematic than the British press. There are, after all, three sports papers to fill each day, and each one has to have more tempting headlines than its rival. Then there are the demanding fans. Football is followed with a passion in Italy that is unequalled anywhere else in the world, except maybe in some South American countries. If the Italian population goes to mass on Sunday morning, they go to watch 'calcio' on Sunday afternoon. And it was at the football ground that the week's frustrations and disappointments are transferred onto the team. If the team play well, then the star players become heroes, but if things go wrong, all hell breaks loose. Fans have been known to turn up at the training ground the following week and insult the players and manager as they come out of the ground, even kicking their shiny new Mazdas and Mercedes. You cannot go into a bar or a restaurant in Italy without the conversation turning to football. This was not limited to the working class, in Italy football is the plaything of the rich. For the club chairmen especially, it is a way of ensuring constant news coverage. It is not an arena to be entered into lightly, but for a top- class footballer it is the best stage in the world.

After the meeting in Rome, we flew back to London with an agreement to continue the negotiations. There remained a big question mark over whether Gazza could handle the pressure of playing in Italy. During the later stages of his Newcastle career, the fans had been getting him down with their constantly high expectations and volatile humour, so how would he cope with the Italian fans and their great passion for the game? Looking on the positive side was Gazza himself, who was eager to try out his skills in Italian football. He was delighted to hear that Lazio had confirmed that they were very interested in buying him. As ex-general manager, Carlo Regalia recalls: 'Lazio wanted to buy Gascoigne as the chairman's brother, Giorgio, wanted him for the club. Giorgio had not got long to live, so his brother was determined that he would have his dream, whatever it cost.'

The price would be high. Tottenham may have been in financial difficulty, but they had no intention of letting one of their prize assets go cheaply. The Tottenham fans adored Gazza and it would be hard enough to explain why he had to be sold, without having the problem of explaining away a less than decent price for him. In fact, all this pressure concerning the finances at White Hart Lane was beginning to eat away at the very heart of the club. Manager Terry Venables recalls, 'I fell out with Irving Scholar because our agreement was that as manager, I would be in complete control of the hiring and firing of the club's players – but then he [Scholar] took over and started making the decisions.'

Terry was desperate to do everything in his power to keep Gascoigne at Tottenham. He was realistic enough to appreciate the financial situation, but he didn't like the way that his authority was being taken away from him. Finally, he told Scholar that the board of directors would just have to go 'over his head' – and thus began the battle for power at Tottenham, with Terry Venables taking a leading role in the future of the club.

With a wealth of experience behind him, Terry was the

ideal man to transform the club. Irving Scholar was in two minds over the potential sale. He knew it made financial sense, but he was loathe to part with such a valuable asset, and a player who had become a hero to the fans.

The Midland Bank and Nat Solomon had no such qualms. They knew that Gazza had to go and in the end their decision determined the outcome of events.

Meanwhile, on the pitch Tottenham were having a good run in the FA Cup, with Gazza making an outstanding contribution. Appearing with a new haircut against Oxford United in the fourth round, he gave a brilliant performance, scoring two of the goals and having a hand in two more as Spurs defeated the second division side 4–2. The first of his goals was one to treasure. Picking up the ball deep in midfield, he saw Paul Walsh in space and picked out his team-mate, went for the return, and then accelerated through the middle of the Oxford defence, ending up wide of the goal yet still managing to beat the goalkeeper and score. It was a memorable moment.

Gazza was also instrumental in the 2–1 win over Portsmouth in the fifth round tie at Fratton Park, scoring both Tottenham goals and running the show. By the time the quarter-finals came round against Notts County on 10 March, most of the dressing room discussion was centred on Tottenham's worsening financial condition, and Gazza's possible move to Italy. But Gazza refused to let this interfere with his performances on the pitch, and against Notts County he helped his side come back from a goal down to triumph 2–1.

'Gazza was a vital part of the team effort,' says manager Terry Venables, reflecting back on the club's FA Cup run that season. 'He was becoming more mature and decisive on the pitch.'

By this time Lazio and Tottenham were close to reaching agreement on the Gazza deal, but the negotiations with Stein and Lazarus concerning the player's conditions were proving more difficult. Carlo Regalia remembers, 'The negotiations with the club were easier than for the player's contract. For the player's contract every word and every line had to be discussed and renegotiated.'

Nevertheless, as the FA Cup semi-final approached, it seemed that the deal would go through, subject to a satisfactory medical, and Spurs were becoming resigned to losing Gazza to more lucrative pastures. On the day of the match, and in spite of rumours to the contrary, Gazza was part of the line-up as the Tottenham side came out at Wembley to meet old rivals, Arsenal. He was as taut as a spring. Terry Venables had never seen him in such a state.

'He was very hyped up, more hyped up than I've ever seen him. When trying to motivate the team, I was finding it difficult to get a word in...'

In the first half, he provided the kind of brilliance that everyone had come to expect from Gazza. His was a virtuoso performance amid the hurly-burly of the midfield battleground. It culminated in a wonderful piece of opportunism as the Spurs maestro scored direct from a free-kick almost 40 yards from goal, the ball curling perfectly around goalkeeper David Seaman into the top corner of the net. For Terry Venables, this was Gazza at his best.

'He came running over to the bench, screaming. He was so happy, I can still picture his face. It was a goal of perfection.'

Gazza was substituted in the second half as he was suffering from the after-effects of his hernia operation, but Spurs went on to win the match 3–1 and reach the final.

By now the contract and the player's terms had been agreed between Spurs and Lazio. The plan was that I would fly with Gazza to Rome the week after the FA Cup final, so he could be presented to the fans at the Olympic stadium before the final home match against Sampdoria. Lazio had agreed to provide a private jet, and I was busy studying ways that we could enter Italy without people knowing – via the North Pole or Australia, for example! The only worry, as the match kicked off, was that it would go to a replay and wreck our plans.

If the semi-final had been Gascoigne's moment of glory, the final was his moment of disaster. He came out onto the Wembley turf for the Spurs showdown with Nottingham Forest like a temperamental racehorse. He was so hyped up he couldn't stand still. With his emotions running high after all the talk about his impending transfer, it was obvious as soon as the match kicked off that the combination of physical and mental pressures was proving to be lethal. Gazza was out of control.

The team plan was that Lineker would play up-front with five players in midfield and four at the back. Everyone in midfield, except Paul, had defensive responsibilities when the opposition had possession. Gascoigne was to be the first player to support the ball over the half-way line as an attacking midfield player.

Once the match started, however, Gascoigne was all over the place, one moment charging up the right wing, the next on the edge of his own penalty area diving into the tackle. He was in a frenzy to perform well, but it was like watching a moving timebomb. An ex-team-mate reckons that if he had got through the first twenty minutes, he would have gone on to do brilliantly well. But it wasn't to be. After he had nearly put his boot through Garry Parker's chest, an incident for which he really should have been sent off, Gazza then committed the fatal foul that was to have serious repercussions on his whole career. As the ball was played towards the Spurs goal, Forest full-back Gary Charles latched onto it and sprinted across the face of the Spurs penalty area. In his path was the onrushing Gazza, who he attempted to sidestep, but not before the Spurs player had clattered recklessly into his opponent. Both players collapsed to the ground, with the Forest player seemingly the worse off. Gazza got up gingerly, and at first it didn't seem that bad. Seconds later, though, he slumped to the ground in obvious agony, clutching his right knee. Spurs physio John Sheridan knew it was bad and rushed on to the pitch, but no-one had the heart to tell Gazza, as they stretchered him off to a waiting ambulance which headed straight to the Wembley stadium hospital complex. Manager Terry Venables recalls, 'His beaming face – alive and rampant with the joys of life after scoring from the free-kick against Arsenal – was a portrayal of devastation here as he was wheeled away to the dressing room. I will never forget it.'

Gazza realized the injury was serious when he questioned John and the physio didn't answer him. Apart from the Spurs staff, one of the first people to see him was Glenn Roeder who had been in the stands with the Gascoigne family. Mum Carol was in tears and Glenn had rushed down to see what was happening. He had terrible problems getting through security, but eventually made it to the hospital area, where he saw club secretary Peter Barnes and asked how bad it was.

'The doctor has just come out and said he's damaged his cruciate. He's going to be out a year.'

'You've got to be kidding,' was Glenn's shocked response.

'We won't tell him now,' Peter Barnes said as he went back into the hospital area. Glenn went to see Gazza and tried to cheer him up, but in those first few moments it seemed as if his career was over.

Carlo Regalia, who had been in the stands to see Lazio's new acquisition play, was too upset to watch the rest of the match, and left for Heathrow airport soon after the incident to catch the first plane back to Rome. It seemed as if Gazza's dream of playing in Rome would never be fulfilled.

Spurs went on to win the FA Cup that day, and as Terry Venables rightly pointed out, it was a tribute to Gazza's popularity that all the players, along with their wives and girl-friends, wanted to go and visit him in hospital with the Cup.

For several days, it appeared that Lazio deal was off. It was a Jewish holiday, so no-one could speak to either Mel Stein or Len Lazarus. In fact, there was no word coming out of either camp. All that we could hope for was that Gazza would make a good recovery and perhaps be back before the year was up. He was in the hands of top London surgeon, John Browett, who was working on repairing the damage at the Princess Grace Hospital in West London. When Browett opened up the knee, he found that both cruciate ligaments were ruptured. The resulting operation involved tightening the damaged ligaments and replacing the torn tissue. It was a long and delicate procedure.

Gazza was still very close to Jimmy Gardner at this stage, and Jimmy had come down from Newcastle to visit his friend in hospital. In spite of the foolishness of the injury, a fact that even Gazza later admitted, his plight had touched the hearts of thousands of people. If it had been a normal bloke who had done something stupid, then everyone would have said what an idiot and left it at that. But this was Gazza, and his vulnerability somehow transcended any normal negative reaction to such a foolhardy act, with the result that he received hundreds of get-well cards, flowers and messages. The whole nation wanted to see the old Gazza back on his feet.

As far as off-the-pitch activities were concerned, his injury obviously put a stop to much of the promotional appearances and this gave him the chance to recover his equilibrium. Strangely enough, once he had got over the shock, he didn't seem too worried about the injury and felt sure he would be back. It was not long before he was up to his old pranks, such as spraying water over the media people camped outside his window. While in hospital, he also had plenty of time to reflect on his past. He even managed to rediscover the joys of dabbling in poetry writing, and as I look back on that period now, there was one particular verse he had penned while in his hospital bed that seemed to sum up the whole situation.

Now what is in my mind right now
No-one will ever know
But when I'm given that big, big chance
It will be a one-man show.

He was right, no-one did know what was in his mind, but those few words summed up his determination to get back to full fitness. He knew he wasn't finished yet, and now he was going to gather all his strength and show us all that the one-man show, the great talent that is Paul Gascoigne, would soon be back. All of us, including Lazio, held our breath and hoped he would be given a second chance to finish what he had only just started. Such talent could not be wasted just yet.

BUON GIORNO, ITALY

The Rome club kept a low profile for a couple of days, while gathering information from surgeon John Browett and physio John Sheridan on the likelihood of Gazza recovering fully from the awful injury. The newspaper headlines suggested that everything would be called off and Gazza would remain a Tottenham player, except that now the club had a huge debt *and* an injured star player.

Behind the scenes at White Hart Lane, things were developing fast. Alan Sugar, a hard-nosed businessman responsible for building Amstrad into a multi-million pound empire, had made a takeover bid for the club with the support of manager Terry Venables. Sugar considered Gazza to be a bit of a nutter and, as a man used to taking measured risks, he wasn't too keen on the fact that he might be losing a precious commodity because of a moment's madness. The £7.5 million that it was agreed Tottenham would receive for Gazza before the fateful injury was now looking like pie in the sky, and even if Gazza regained full fitness there would have to be a renegotiation of terms. So having originally agreed on a fee and concluded the deal in Gianmarco Calleri's office in Rome, everything was set for the transfer to go ahead – then came the Wembley injury.

On the Wednesday after the FA Cup final, after he had been assured that a full recovery was a good possibility, Calleri turned up at the Princess Grace Hospital to see the injured star and bring him an early birthday present of a £7,000 wristwatch, which Gazza gave to his Dad. It was now obvious to the world that Lazio's goodwill in the deal had never been in question and that they were still interested. Further negotiations started to discuss a reduction in price, and a revision of other terms. Lazio proposed that the original price of £7.5 million be reduced to £4.7 million. However, this was not the final figure paid. Since the original agreement had been drawn up, Terry Venables had brought into the discussions Gino Santin, a restaurateur and friend who had experience of football transfer negotiations through working for AC Milan in their deals with Luther Blissett,Ray Wilkins and Mark Hateley. Santin managed to get the price up to £5.5 million, which ended up as £6.2 million once the interest and money from the two pre-arranged Lazio versus Tottenham ties were taken into account. Some of the terms in the player's contract were also revised, but this time with both Stein and Lazarus, according to Carlo Regalia, 'being easier to deal with'. In a further bid to ease the financial situation at Tottenham, a deal taking Gary Lineker to Japanese side Grampus Eight was signed and paid for a year before he was due to join his club out in the Far East.

Though Gazza himself was keen to play abroad, he had been slightly disappointed that Tottenham had not moved heaven and earth to keep him. He had been trembling when he went to tell Terry Venables that he wanted to go to Lazio, but Terry had taken him aside and said he understood. He knew that the Italian club were offering Gazza a fortune and he wouldn't be able to hold the player back. Gazza may have been in the middle of his contract, but the London club were in no financial state to hang on to him.

Throughout the post-Wembley manoeuvres, the papers had reckoned without the determination of Lazio chairman, Gianmarco Calleri. As well as wanting to buy Gascoigne for his brother, Calleri was well aware of Gazza's star quality. For

Lazio, Gascoigne wasn't just a highly talented player, he was also an international star, and would be good for the club's worldwide image. The complexities of Italian football are such that a player isn't just bought for his playing abilities but also for his 'pulling' power. It was thought that with Gazza being such a character and having the kind of personality that attracts attention, he would be a good draw in arranging international friendlies and pushing the club back to the forefront of European football. For too long, Lazio had been in the shadow of their Roman cousins AS Roma, and now they wanted to make a concerted effort to be back in the limelight. However, it would have been easy for Lazio to go chasing another star footballer, and it is to Calleri's credit that he showed such loyalty to Gazza, a loyalty which Gazza would be determined to repay.

By the summer, it was all back on. Gazza went on holiday with his Dad, his sister's boyfriend, John Paul, best friend Jimmy 'Five Bellies', and of course his faithful physio John Sheridan, who had dedicated himself to getting Gazza back on his feet. They set off to Portugal and John Sheridan remembers: 'Gazza was very positive, he worked very hard on his exercises during the holiday and made a lot of progress. He loves football and he wanted to play again. My job was to give him a functional knee.' John organized a series of aqua exercises for Gazza to start work on building up the leg muscles supporting the knee.

Things were going pretty smoothly, apart from the odd minor incident such as the time Gazza's sister was attacked in a Newcastle street. Our intrepid hero had rushed to her support, but unfortunately lashed out at the man who was attempting to assist – and promptly ended up on an assault charge! However, this did not seem to deter Gazza in his single-minded pursuit of getting back to full fitness. He knew that Lazio were on his side, and this was important in his fightback to recovery. Paul has always valued loyalty very highly on his list of attributes for friends and family, and he

Three faces of Paul Gascoigne – as a promising 18-year-old at Newcastle (*above*), a £2 million purchase by Spurs in 1988 (*right*) and England's saviour at the 1990 World Cup in Italy (*below*).

During Italia 90, Gazza established himself as one of the stars of the tournament, despite the presence of European Footballer of the Year, Marco Van Basten (*left*) and West Germany's captain, Lothar Matthaus (*below*).

A sad farewell to the land of the lira after England's heroic but unsuccessful showing against West Germany in the World Cup semi-final.

'Bobby Robson never complained that I was overweight!' (*left*). Meanwhile, some photo opportunities are just too good to miss! (*below*).

Two average, law-abiding members of the England squad (*below*), with of course not a bottle in sight!

What a GOAL! Arsenal v Spurs, 1991 FA Cup semi-final at Wembley.

Gascoigne and Lineker (*below*) receiving end-of season awards for Spurs, alongside Alan Sugar, Terry Venables and Tony Berry, all three of whom would come under the microscope in the years ahead.

The tackle on Gary Charles during the 1991 FA Cup final. A moment of complete and utter madness.

Spurs physios John Sheridan and Dave Butter attend to Gazza's wrecked knee.

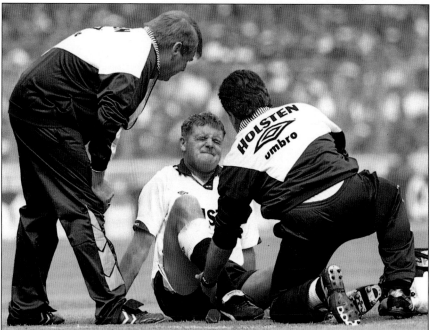

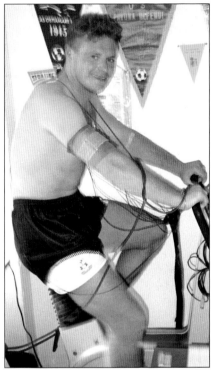

The long road back to full recovery. Gazza leaving Princess Grace Hospital in Marylebone (*above*) and putting on a brave face (*right*) during the arduous fitness tests in Rome.

'Italy, here I come!' Flying out to Rome in August 1991.

Taking in the sights with Mel Stein and Gazza's best mate, Glenn Roeder.

The Gascoigne party (*from left to right*): Dad, Minder 1 Gianni Zeqireya, John Sheridan, Mr X himself, and Minder 2 Augusto Perotti.

With Mick and Lazio team-mate Thomas Doll.

Gingerly inspecting the troublesome knee during a Lazio training session.

'Anything Vinny Jones can do, I can do better.' Gazza getting to grips with Lazio goalkeeper Nando Orsi.

felt that he had to repay the faith that Lazio were placing in him. Apart from that, Gazza was demonstrating the strength of his willpower in the face of adversity, a trait that was in clear evidence to those around him at this time.

'It is to Gazza's great credit that he has played again,' says John Sheridan. 'His was one of the worst injuries I have had to work on, and some footballers wouldn't have kicked a ball again. The fact that he is playing again is down to several things, the most important being his great love of football and his dedication to get fit and play again. He also had a good surgeon in John Browett and, fortunately, his body heals quite quickly.'

John Sheridan's role in the fightback to recovery was crucial. As one of the football world's most experienced physiotherapists, he was the ideal person to see Gazza through the trauma of his injury and provide expert advice through the rehabilitation period. He has since opened his own clinic in Luton, specializing in sports injuries.

It was also a bit of a honeymoon period with the press. As Gazza wasn't playing, they weren't hounding him so much and he found that he liked being out of the spotlight and allowed to get on with his life without the daily grind of avoiding the press and carrying out his other engagements. Suddenly, he also found that the commercial pressure was off, as he was limited in what he could do. No-one could expect him to visit exhibitions and trade fairs if he had a bad knee and should be resting.

His private life was still quite lively. Sheryl Kyle, along with a number of others, was still on the scene. Their relationship hadn't yet developed into anything serious, but she was still very much in touch and as she lived near him, it wasn't difficult for them to see each other. Sheryl was in considerable financial difficulty following husband Colin's declaration of bankruptcy. As he wasn't paying her any maintenance money, she risked having her house repossessed through not being able to keep up with the mortgage payments. Paul, however, was always available to help. Sheryl herself has said that sometimes she would find a bag of groceries on her doorstep from him, and other little signs of concern. His naturally giving nature would not have allowed a woman and two children to suffer, if he could help in any way.

In August, Lazio were confident enough that Paul Gascoigne soon would be on their books, that they invited him down to Rome to attend an important friendly match with Real Madrid. It was a match that had been organized in memory of chairman Calleri's deceased brother, Giorgio, and Calleri was very keen to have Paul present, especially as his brother had wanted Paul as part of the team. It was on the Friday of the August bank holiday weekend, so it was arranged that everyone would fly down to Rome on the day, and there would be a press conference on arrival followed by the match.

At that time, the assumption was that Gazza would commute between London and Rome during the remainder of his recuperation period, and therefore, one of my briefs was to find a place for him to live, as well as a place for Glenn, Faith, Holly and William, who would move out to Italy with him. The plan was that we would also look for suitable schools for Holly and a nursery school for William. The trip to Rome was to be Paul's initiation into Roman culture, and a chance for us to lay a few foundations for his future with Lazio.

Ever since the Gazza bandwagon started to roll, Mel Stein and Len Lazarus had employed a PA to arrange their client's various appointments and keep tabs on his whereabouts day and night. This wasn't as easy as it first appeared as Gazza wasn't always willing to participate in every commercial venture arranged for him. The first poor person to take on the role was Len Lazarus' sister-in-law, Renée. Trying to keep track of Gazza nearly drove her round the bend, and she soon gave up. The person who replaced her was a girl called Jane Featherstone, a bright, likeable graduate who was looking for work experience. In fact, Jane handled the various elements of the job – the sponsors, advertisers, journalists and even Gazza himself – with considerable diplomacy and, with a good sense of humour. Moreover, she was paid very little for it. When Jane left, I was brought in not only to be Gazza's PA in Rome but also to build up the commercial side of the business in Italy through bringing in sponsors and advertising deals. However, my brief stopped at the financial negotiations, which were handled exclusively by Mel Stein and Len Lazarus on behalf of Gazza.

The auspices were not particularly good as we travelled to the airport on that sunny day in August for our flight out to Rome. A minor incident occurred on the way – a police van, of all things, had run into my hired car, something which could only happen when Gazza was about. Apart from that, things proceeded relatively smoothly. The official party consisted of Gazza, his Dad, Glenn, a crew from Chrysalis who were filming 'Gazza – the fightback', Mel, his wife Marilyn and their two sons, Nicky and Paul, and Dave Smith of *Shoot* magazine. There was also a group of journalists in tow.

On arriving at the airport, Gazza was whisked away, amid hundreds of flashbulbs, to the VIP lounge, and was not seen again until escorted by two police officers on to the plane. Once on board, Gazza was between his Dad and Glenn. He was in a buoyant mood ('The plane's overloaded, chuck out the Harry Harris!' he shouted referring to the *Daily Mirror* Chief Sports Writer). John Gascoigne was looking rather nervous as he took his seat, since he hated flying. You could see some of Paul in his Dad, the shape of the face and the similar nose. Paul had also inherited some of his father's talent. John used to play football, not as a professional, but he was a reasonably good amateur player. He was the gentle, sensitive parent (when I once suggested that his son needed a good hiding, John looked at me and said, 'I couldn't hit them when they were bairns, let alone now'), but he showed a quiet stubbornness when it came to wanting something for his family. He was a great influence on Paul and clearly there was a strong bond of affection between the two. Carol Gascoigne, Paul's mum, had a more fiery and determined personality, and it was from her that Paul inherited the iron will to overcome his difficulties. John had suffered from a brain haemorrhage when Paul was eleven, and it was left to Carol to bring up the four children and be the breadwinner until John received. But his parents are vital to his happiness and success and it is to them that he turns to when the going gets tough.

John Gascoigne was someone who represented stability. He didn't tolerate fools gladly and could spot a sponger from a hundred miles away. A man of few words, John was one of the few people who, when necessary, could control his son. He was also a person who would do anything for you, just like the rest of Paul's family, who were a generous, down-to-earth group of people who happened to have found a superstar in their midst. But he's never forgotten his roots, even when external forces would try and tear him away from his close-knit and loving family. This was something that changed their lives as well as his. They were financially better off, but at a cost to them of their mental tranquillity. Now they had to be careful of the press and constantly aware of who they could trust. Carol also had her share of sleepless nights worrying about her much-loved son, and the people, particularly the girls, with whom he had been involved.

With the presence of such a big group, the flight was soon turned into a small party, with an atmosphere full of hope and expectation as we landed. The first inkling we had of the welcome that was in store for us, was when the captain made an announcement: 'Would Mr Gascoigne's group please remain on board.'

A few seconds later, a couple of policemen together with Lazio team manager, Maurizio Manzini, appeared on the plane. Apparently, airport employees, who were also Lazio fans, were waiting outside the plane to greet their hero, in the usual noisy and enthusiastic Italian way. We were hustled down the plane steps and on to a special bus, and as soon as Gazza was safely inside, the doors quickly shut tight, and the fans were left to bang on the windows and shout Gazza's name. Having lived in Italy for some time, I was not totally surprised by this open display of adoration, but Marilyn Stein was alarmed by what appeared to be totally uncontrolled hero worship. It wasn't over yet.

Arriving at passport control, it was decided that Glenn and Mel would stay with Gazza and the rest of us would go straight through to the waiting cars and on to the Hilton hotel. Eventually, after much flapping about, a couple of policemen were attached to us and we were whisked through passport control, without so much as the colour of our passports being questioned. Immediately on the other side of passport control, there were a group of twenty or so journalists and television crews. There seemed to be general chaos all round.

We collected our bags and headed expectantly for the exit. It sounded like a pack of wild animals on the other side of the screen.

'Paul Gascoigne La La La La La La,
Paul Gascoigne La La La La La La.'

As we emerged, our faces dropped. Lined up from the ceiling to the floor and standing on each others shoulders, were thousands of hysterical Lazio fans. Our senses were hit by a sea of light blue and white. It was like being hit by a giant wave, so colourful and so noisy that it almost took our breath away. When the fans spotted us and realized we were part of the Gascoigne entourage, they all strained forward to get a closer look, nearly breaking the fragile barrier of police protecting us.

It was something that I had never witnessed before or since in connection with football – an amazing experience. After escaping from the airport concourse, we were hustled into the Mondiapol cars and driven away at top speed to the

Hilton. A few minutes after our arrival, the superstar himself arrived with Glenn Roeder and Mel Stein – all of them shaken, but not stirred. Gazza had turned up with two bodyguards, Gianni and Augusto, provided by Calleri's security firm, Mondiapol. Both were big lads and used to dealing with megastars. Augusto had been Madonna's bodyguard on her recent concert appearance in Rome, while Gianni would become a close friend of Paul's during their time in Italy.

Paul just had time to shower and change, before the whole circus moved down to the press conference, where Calleri and his colleagues were waiting for us, to show their acquisition off to the world. Paul seemed in a very good mood; he was buoyed by the warmth of the fans and happy to see so many people come and greet him. He wasn't too keen on press conferences, but here he was unusually relaxed and at peace with his surroundings. It was suggested that the English party should make a low-key entrance from a side door. The Italians thought this was ridiculous and insisted we all make our grand appearance through the main door. As a result, we ended up as an untidy rabble by the stage, blinking like foxes caught in car headlights, as flashbulbs went off around us.

Gazza taking all this in his stride, promptly put on his silly glasses and planted a huge kiss on Calleri's cheek. It wasn't an entirely serious affair, but then nobody expected it to be. There were at least a dozen television crews in the room, plus a hundred or so journalists from all over Italy. Gazza was big news, even if he hadn't kicked a ball for several months. His larger-than-life personality attracted the Italians, who appreciated celebrity status and exuberant personalities. During one of the question-and-answer sessions, an attractive looking reporter from Telemontecarlo asked him if he preferred to be called Paul or Gazza. 'Paul *before* you go to bed with me, Gazza *after*,' he cheekily replied amid nervous titters of appreciation. It was only on the subject of football that he was serious. Lazio had shown their loyalty to him throughout the recuperation period, and he was going to pay it back by not only getting fit but by proving he was worth every penny of the money the club was spending on him. 'I want to play for Lazio, and I'll be back on top soon,' was his battle cry.

After this was over, we had a couple of hours to relax before going to the Olympic stadium. As I stood on the balcony of my room, I was witness to an extraordinary scene in which a couple of photographers had climbed trees in the grounds to try and get offbeat photos of Gazza, and were being chased by the hotel security men. A couple of minutes later, Gazza appeared on his balcony and waved to them, then before they had time to lift their cameras he disappeared. It was reminiscent of the type of interest that a pop star generates, and as I stood there I wondered how he would react when the results were bad and the pressure on. He usually got twitchy when under media pressure; if they were climbing trees to get to him now, what would they be doing if he didn't perform well?

Bringing Paul to the stadium in this atmosphere of hysteria was already complicated, yet it wasn't the only problem. The Jewish Sabbath had started, which meant that Mel Stein couldn't use any form of motorized transport. It meant he had to go to the Olympic stadium on foot (a good hours walk!), so we arranged to all meet up there.

The Olympic stadium, with its impressive oval, low-slung shape, resembled a spaceship settling in amongst the greenery of northern Rome. As we approached the long driveway up to the main entrance, hundreds of fans ran up to greet Gazza and shout his name through the windows of the car. Even the policemen and traffic wardens on duty all joined in the fun and started waving and blowing their whistles. He waved to them happily from the back of the Mercedes and moments later we were in the underground car park next to the team bus.

In the team dressing room, Gazza was introduced to his new team-mates and manager Dino Zoff, under the guidance of Maurizio Manzini who spoke very good English. Introductions were cordial and polite. The Italians were intrigued by all the hype surrounding this much talked-about star, and were interested to find out how he was getting over his knee injury. On his part, Gazza was curious to hear all about Italian football. The Lazio goalkeeper, Valerio Fiori, and midfield player, Claudio Sclosa, both spoke English, so they acted as spokesmen for the rest of the team.

After the dressing room, it was decided to present Gazza to the fans, so we gathered at the steps leading up to the pitch and waited. Above us, we could hear the roar of the crowd, but we had no idea how many fans were there. All we could see was a mass of photographers at the top of the steps. 'Keep back, mind his knee,' Manzini shouted as he went up the steps on to the pitch.

Bodyguards Gianni and Augusto prepared themselves to protect their charge. Although big blokes, this was a challenge even for them. In the middle of all this, Gazza was standing quietly to one side with Glenn. He didn't seem nervous or uptight, just watchful. At last, up went Gazza and the flashbulbs started going, and the fans went wild. On the huge display screen, a video of Gazza singing 'Fog on the Tyne' and 'Geordie Boys' appeared. Everyone started singing along.

The whole of the Lazio terrace was packed with fans buried under a mountain of scarves, flags and banners. *Gazza's men are here to stay, shag women, drink beer, ...,* was on one of the colourful banners. Obviously the fans had summed him up fairly accurately, even if the management thought differently. Surrounded by a cordon of photographers, Gazza ran towards the terraces, at which point the fans all began chanting his name and waving their banners. It was a touching moment and an indication of how much he was loved, even though he hadn't set foot in Italy since the World Cup. The fans wanted a big personality who would lead the club out of the doldrums. Lazio hadn't played in the European cup competitions since the 1977/78 season and they were always finishing below arch-rivals AS Roma in the league. Things had to change.

Gazza ran round the stadium and was greeted as a hero by all the fans, as they stood and cheered. He was clearly moved by the reception and at the end, he ran back down the steps and stood for a few seconds trying to recover his breath and composure. 'Unbelievable!' was his only word as the sights and sounds continued to buzz round his head.

The night had been about the triumphant entry of Paul Gascoigne into the arena of Italian football. After the match, we all returned to at the Hilton and had dinner on the terrace by the swimming pool. Chairman Gianmarco Calleri bought along some of the VIP fans, including Italian comic actor Enrico Montesano. It had been a perfect start to Gazza's Roman adventure.

As Gazza settled into his seat to eat his dinner, he was still on a high after the welcome he had received from the fans. 'It was just incredible, it made me feel really wanted, it was just great,' he smiled as he tucked into his mozzarella and salami.

A couple of days later, we went on a tour round Rome to see the sights. It was a chance for Gazza to catch up on the cultural side of the city. We did all the usual things that tourists do and went to the Trevi Fountain, place of Anita Ekberg's triumphant appearance in *La Dolce Vita*, and visited the historical centre, just as Audrey Hepburn had done in *Roman Holiday*. One of Gazza's favourite places was the Bocca della Verita, which consisted of a Medusa-like stone face in the wall with a hole in the mouth. Tradition goes that if you are a liar, your hand will be cut off if you place it in the mouth. Gazza put his hand in the mouth, then pulled his sleeve down to cover his hand and grinned mischievously. He got his Dad and Glenn to do the 'test' as well.

I had never seen Gazza so relaxed as during this period. Even though the hysterical fans at the airport had been frightening, he had got through that experience well. The press conference, another potential banana skin, had been a breeze, and here he was wandering around sightseeing like thousands of others. At night, he had two burly minders who slept in the next room with a connecting door, so he didn't have to worry about his personal safety. Even more important, he had best mate Glenn Roeder at his side. Glenn had been through everything with him and was someone he could trust and also someone who would guide him in the right direction. Dad John was around as the stabilizing factor. Mel Stein, Gazza's trusted business adviser and protector, was there to take any media pressure off him and absorb any requests from the club. And I was there, at Mel's suggestion, to help him sort out the practical side of things. So all he had to do was enjoy himself, knowing that there was always someone about to either entertain him, or run around for him.

Moreover, he wasn't emotionally tied to any woman, so he didn't have to keep dashing off to check-up on what she was up to back home. In fact, he was having a whale of a time boozing and clubbing. His poor minders, Gianni and Augusto, had managed to catch about two hours' sleep in two days as they accompanied him on his nightly forays into Rome. One evening, towards the end of his stay, Gazza had met up with a man called Massimo (not my future boyfriend!) who had brought along two local women to entertain himself and Gazza, one of whom was particularly striking, a dyed-blonde dressed in skin-tight, black stretch trousers with wide lacing up the sides. The last sighting of the group that night was one of a bedraggled mob heading towards the nearest hostelry – without Glenn Roeder, I should add, who had stayed in the hotel.

The only thing that slightly bothered Gazza during his Roman escapades was the photographers. He was very keen to be seen doing his exercises and working, not just running around playing table tennis and swimming in the pool, so he avoided the photographers as much as possible. However, he did something later in the week that, if it had been photographed would have caused a worldwide sensation.

Dad John had confided in me that he had been a bit worried about his son's nocturnal habits, so we decided to dash off to the local chemist and buy a packet of condoms for Gazza to take with him at night, just in case the need arose. On the way back to the hotel, John said quite seriously, 'Don't say you bought them or he'll be embarrassed.'

We got back and found Gazza, Glenn, Gianni and Augusto, having lunch. John quietly slipped the paper bag to Paul, while John and I, together with my friend Tiziana Maestrelli, whose father was the last manager to lead Lazio to the league title, sat down at another table. As we were ordering our food, we heard a few giggles and looked up. There was Gazza sitting at his table, looking at us with the widest of grins on his face ... and with a blown-up condom on his head! It was a hot day in August and the swimming pool area was crowded with families enjoying a quiet, relaxing lunch. Everyone seemed a bit surprised to see a foreign bloke sitting at the table with a condom on his head. However, in typical Italian style they all had a good laugh, composed themselves, and then went back to the more important pastime of eating. They probably thought it was some strange English habit to put a condom on your head after lunch. They certainly must have wondered about the standard of sex education in English schools.

Gazza, however, hadn't finished. When the group got up to leave the outdoor restaurant area, the condom went back on his head as he grinned at us from behind the plate glass windows separating the two sections of the restaurant. And this from a person who is terrified of photographers! Whether the condoms were ever used for their true purpose was never established, as I never saw Miss 'Lace-up Trousers' and her friend again.

On the bank holiday Monday, most of our entourage disappeared back to England, leaving Gazza, John Gascoigne, Glenn and myself out in Rome. It hadn't been decided as to when we would go back to England as Gazza seemed to be enjoying himself so much. At last, he was among people who adored him for what he was, and didn't build him up only to knock him down again. He loved all aspects of the Italian way of life, and even developed a taste for the food, in particular Mozzarella, which he would eat until it came out of his ears.

Every day, we all used to meet up on the terrace at the hotel to enjoy the lunch buffet, which was full of colourful and appetizing food like ham, salami, lobster and every kind of salad imaginable. Gazza loved it. During his time at Tottenham he would pig out on the food at every opportunity, so much so that he would have to retreat to the gents and throw up. One of his Spurs team-mates had taught him the trick and Gazza thought this way he could keep his weight down, and keep Tottenham happy and be able to enjoy his food at the same time. He'd found the ideal way to literally have his cake and eat it then throw up, and that would mean he would stay the same weight. However, he hadn't considered the debilitating effect of such behaviour.

In the meantime, I had started running around looking for villas with Tiziana. We also visited all the international schools and spoke to the various head teachers in search of the right one. By the end of the week, we had found a suitable villa near Formello, where the new Lazio training ground is being built, and about twenty minutes from the existing training ground. We had also selected St George's international school as the likely place of education for Holly, and eventually William. The villa was ideal; there were five bedrooms on three floors, a massive swimming pool with a changing area out back, a games room, a barbecue, etc. John and I went along to see it first and John thought it would be suitable. Paul and Glenn came along a few days later and Paul fell in love with it immediately. The villa next door even had it's own five-a-side football pitch, so it was perfect in all aspects. Moreover, the cost of renting it per month was a reasonable one for a villa of this quality. We shook hands with the owner and agreed to discuss furnishing it later.

The school was also agreed, with Faith saying that she would come and see it when Glenn was next out in Rome. Things seemed to be falling perfectly into place. Glenn loved it in Italy as well. For him it was the chance to broaden his horizons and get involved with another culture. He had played football at the highest level and now he was to come out to Rome, initially to look after Gazza, but also to gain experience of the international football.

If Gazza was suited to playing in Italy, Glenn was suited to the management side. Glenn not only had a wealth of experience, but he also had the communication skills and intelligence to use it. He wanted to learn Italian so he could speak to people like Zoff and talk football with them. Although modesty wouldn't allow him to admit it, Glenn Roeder would have made the perfect international adviser for any Italian club.

He had been very impressed with what he saw on his trip to Rome with Gazza. Glenn loved everything, – the professionalism, the match preparation, the way they train, the attitude of the players, the way they live, and how they looked after themselves. When Lazio went down to Bari to play third division team Andria in the Italian cup, Glenn and Gazza went along as well. What Glenn saw left a lasting memory.

'The stadium was packed, there were about twelve thousand fans, all Andria fans. It was a white hot atmosphere, there were fireworks, the lot. It was a difficult game to win, but Lazio managed it. After the match, we all went back to the team hotel. Now, if that had been an English team they would have celebrated all night; half the team wouldn't have gone to bed at all, and the other half would have had about two hour's sleep. The next morning they would have all crawled on to the team coach bleary-eyed. The Lazio players had their meal, went upstairs to the lounge area of the hotel, had coffee and a quiet walk around the hotel gardens. They were all in bed, without being asked, within an hour of the meal finishing. Everyone was on the coach the next morning, bills paid, smart blazers and ties all in place, ready to go to the airport, ten minutes before the coach was due to leave. Their level of self-discipline was astonishing. It made me feel ashamed. I have played football for twenty years and it has never been like that in my experience of the English game.

'When England plays Italy, there is an equal chance of either side beating the other. Over ten games, the Italians will probably beat us more times. If the English lived like the Italians we would have won the World Cup three or four times. It's amazing what we do achieve taking into consideration our lifestyle. But just think what we could achieve if we lived like the Italians.'

This philosophy continued at the training ground. During training sessions Glenn changed next to Cristiano Bergodi, Lazio's right-back.

'He is a right-back, so he cannot be the most highly paid player, but he comes to the training ground in a beautiful new Mercedes and appreciates it. He tells me they train, go home, and have a siesta. An English player would train, go straight into Rome and walk round the shops, no matter how hot it was. But this is part of their mentality, it is the way they are brought up. There must be one or two playboys, but on the whole, they live lives adapted to being a top-class athlete.'

Towards the end of the trip, I was caught on the end of a Paul Gascoigne joke. One evening, he called me over to where he was sitting in a circle with his dad, Glenn, Gianni and Augusto. He explained that we were all going to play this game whereby you had to copy the actions of the person sitting on your right, for example someone would start if off by touching your cheek, you had to repeat this, then you would pinch the cheek, touch the forehead etc. Anyone who made a mistake had to have a drink. I arrived with my ex-boyfriend and his dad, and Gazza made me sit next to him. The game had gone on for some time, when I realized that he had an ashtray in his hand, and a hand full of ash! My face was black and I had to walk through the Hilton looking like a chimney sweep! I suppose at least it was a sign that I was considered one of the boys.

The big question was how would Gazza fit into the disciplined lifestyle? During the trip, Gazza went out with goalkeepers Fiori and Orsi. He got drunk, they didn't. The next day they wanted to know if he was always like that, and if it affected his health. The conversation had turned from football to health. It was a sign of things to come.

On our return from Italy, it seemed as if everything was on schedule for the whole Gazza bandwaggon to move out to Rome within a month. The villa contract had been drawn up, and the school booked. I had negotiated with Mel and Len regarding the terms of my contract, which provided me with a flat, also to be used as an office; paid the running expenses of my car; and which arranged that I be paid £15 per hour, with a monthly retainer of £1,500 plus a bonus on commercial contracts of 5% if I'd arranged them myself or 2.5% through another company. The Paul Gascoigne Promotions office, or PGP, Rome, was put into motion. Everything was ready – and then disaster struck.

At the end of September, Paul decided to go up to Newcastle to see his friends and family. He promised Glenn that he would be sensible and would not stray further than the Dunston Working Men's Club. However, in the afternoon he decided to go and watch Newcastle play and followed this by hitting the town in the evening. He ended up in a nightclub with friend Jimmy Gardner, where they had a few drinks before Jimmy went home, leaving Paul with other friends. It was then that he was struck by a complete stranger while coming out of the gents, and in the scuffle that followed his knee was injured. The first that Jimmy knew about it was when Gazza turned up on his doorstep in the early hours of the morning, looking white and with his knee cap displaced. Jimmy immediately dropped everything and rushed him straight to see John Sheridan, who took one look at the knee and contacted John Browett. Once again John Browett was to miss his Sunday lunch.

The first I knew of the incident was when Mel Stein rang

me on Sunday morning to say that Gazza was injured, in hospital, and as it was about to be a three-day Jewish holiday, it was over to me. Another major Gazza injury and another Jewish holiday, were the two things connected? I was due to go up to Birmingham the next day, so I left my mother to hold the fort, and disappeared off. John Browett was left wondering if we were all crackers when he tried to phone me and got my rather harassed mother, inadvertently informing him that I was rather busy, followed by a call to Mel Stein, who said it was a Jewish holiday, that he couldn't talk and put the phone down. He must have wondered if anyone wanted to claim his notorious patient. Meanwhile, Gazza was in the depths of depression. He knew he shouldn't have gone to the nightclub, and he was now wondering if his career really was over.

Initially, Gazza had wanted to press charges, but then changed his mind. It was this turnaround that sparked off the rumours in the press that he had injured himself through having too much to drink. In an interview with the *Sun* on 6 August, Jimmy 'Five Bellies' spoke out.

'That [the incident] was all caused by jealousy. When Paul left Newcastle for Spurs, people in his home city turned against him. It was disgusting.'

I phoned him on Monday afternoon from Birmingham airport, and said I would be in to see him the next day. The following afternoon, I went to the Princess Grace hospital with Jane Featherstone and Neil Duncanson from Chrysalis television. We found a joke shop near the hospital and stocked up on some silly gifts. Paul seemed pretty down when we arrived, he was very subdued and not at all his usual bubbly self. He said he had been hit and showed us the cracked tooth that he suffered from the thump on the jaw. The thug had followed up by kicking his right leg. This was now laying on a support, the knee cap broken. It was back to square one for Gazza. The one good thing was that no further damage had been done to the cruciate ligaments. John Sheridan was displaying caution.

'I had to reschedule his programme. Before the second

injury the knee was eighty per cent back to full movement. Now we had to be careful with the patella, and bring in another set of exercises to take this into consideration. They were two different injuries, so it was back to the beginning.'

Tottenham were far from happy at the second injury, and Alan Sugar was furious as he believed that the club might be left with egg on its face and no money if Gazza wrecked his knee for good. In his mind, there was now no question of Gazza leaving White Hart Lane.

It wasn't the physical aspect of the injury that had done most damage. It was the emotional blow that had hit Gazza for six. Even in his Newcastle playing days, he had a difficult relationship with the Tyneside public. Seen as a larger-than-life character, there were many people who wanted to put him in his place. It seemed to be symptomatic of the place that if you were doing well, they wanted to take you down a peg or two.

However, yet another shock was in store for Gazza. His friend and mentor, Glenn Roeder, suddenly decided to pull out of the deal to accompany him to Rome. Glenn was a very straightforward, honest person and he admitted to feeling badly let down by Paul's actions over the past few months, especially over the punch-up incident. He felt that if Paul wouldn't take his advice now, then it would be hopeless in Rome.

It was a decision that was to cost Glenn a lot, both in emotional terms – after all he was turning his back on a friend who he had seen develop from the Newcastle youth team to international stardom – and in financial terms, as it was to be a long time before he managed to get another job. He'd also just had an operation on his achilles tendon to enable him to take part in the Lazio training sessions. It would have been a big thrill for him to play on the same field as international stars like Karlheinz Riedle, Thomas Doll, Aron Winter and Beppe Signori. Yet he was prepared to give it all up and allow his dream to sink into the ground.

Glenn Roeder felt the time had come to take a moral stand-point – his integrity was very much at stake. In the past, others had tried to help Gazza mend his ways, without success. But Glenn's departure from his life was to have devastating consequences. Maybe no-one realized just how emotionally dependent he was on the calm and orderly lives of the Roeder family. For years, ever since he had been at Newcastle, Glenn and Faith had been there for him. He'd drop in and out, with no warning, and sometimes stay the night if he felt like it. He was always welcome, and even though he sometimes stretched to the limit the hospitality offered him by turning up with various women at all times of the day and night, he was never refused entry. Suddenly, he felt he was being cast out just when he was at his most vulnerable, and he couldn't handle it.

Glenn could not be blamed for pulling out. He had to think of his wife and family and he couldn't build his family's future on Gazza's unpredictability. He just couldn't risk a disaster in a foreign country. There were no hard feelings towards Paul, and Glenn wanted to maintain their friendship, but Gazza never contacted him from Rome and so as time wore on they drifted apart.

As a result of Glenn Roeder's decision, however, Gazza became more dependent on Sheryl Kyle. Within a few weeks Sheryl had become one of the major influences in Gazza's life. In one easy step he'd swopped the easy, loving atmosphere of the Roeder's house in Essex for the second family he found with Sheryl.

Like the Roeders, Sheryl had two kids, daughter Bianca Jade and son Mason. Paul needed Sheryl and her kids to help balance his insecurity and satisfy his need for emotional fulfilment. But there would be a high price to pay. His relationship with her moved from being just good friends to becoming exclusive lovers when she returned from holiday after his second injury in October 1991. He said he wanted her to be special and not surprisingly, she agreed. It was to be some time before they would go out in public as a couple, but they started to spend a great deal of time together, and she started to influence his decisions.

Throughout all this, Lazio still remained steadfast in their determination to buy Paul Gascoigne. The day that I called into the hospital, they had turned up in London to talk to the doctors. It was a strange transfer deal; they spent more time talking to doctors than talking to the club from whom they were buying the player. Once again, John Browett had put Humpty Dumpty together again, and had assured Lazio that his recovery should be delayed only by about six weeks. However, if he fell off the wall again, it was quite likely that Humpty Dumpty's body would shatter into a thousand pieces and be swept away for good. Luckily, Gazza seemed to get the message. He realized he had let everyone down and was determined to settle down with John Sheridan and once again work on getting back to full fitness.

Finally, 1991 came to an end, marked down as the year Gazza nearly ended it all. Negotiations continued into 1992 with Tottenham and with Mel Stein and Len Lazarus. I had to cancel the school place for Holly and let the villa and the office go. Instead, I went back to Rome to try and drum up business on the commercial side. By December, there were a few opportunities but nothing that justified me being in Rome full time, so I went to Glasgow and wrote my second novel and worked on a television series.

The next trip to Rome was for the Lazio versus AS Roma derby match on 1 March 1992. Negotiations for Gazza's contract were still going on, but agreement had nearly been reached. The big difference was that the Lazio management was changing. Gianmarco Calleri was selling his share of the company to international financier Sergio Cragnotti, who had merchant banks in Paris, Milan and London, and a long career as a successful businessman with Ferruzzi, one of the biggest companies in Italy.

Calleri had been responsible for putting Lazio's affairs in

good order. When he had taken over the club, it had been heading towards financial ruin. Rome is the political centre of Italy, and as such, is not surprisingly full of politicians. This meant that every week, thousands of people thought they had the divine right of a free seat at the Olympic stadium, or the Flaminia stadium which is where Lazio used to play. Every minor minister and every head of every tiny police station in Italy thought they should be on a permanent freebie. Predictably, this had disastrous consequences for the balance sheet, so Calleri had come along and quite simply put a stop to it. It made him unpopular, but it had to be done. When he left the club the balance sheets, if not the public relations was back in shape.

The person who now took over the negotiations for Gazza was Lionello Celon, the new managing director of Lazio. An experienced accountant and Cragnotti's right-hand man, he told me did not have an easy time of things with Mel Stein and Len Lazarus. It seems Lazio were having extreme difficulty in agreeing to a request concerning the need for Paul to have a trout breeding centre near his house. It seemed like a minor issue but it became a major point in the negotiation. One could just imagine the discussions – Mel: 'I'll concede the trout farm if you agree to another half a million pounds…' Lazio: 'How about a goldfish bowl?', or something to that effect.

Meanwhile, the derby match was approaching. I arrived a couple of days before the rest of the crowd and was met by Maurizio Manzini. Maurizio as team manager was an important part of the club, he not only organized travel and did the administration relating to the players, but he also acted as a kind of team co-ordinator, arranging for the players to attend fan club dinners, sorting out their various problems.

John Gascoigne and his friend Mick arrived the next day from Newcastle by car. Mick was a nice chap, very easy going and laid-back. We drove into Rome and had steak and veg in the residence that we were all staying in. The following day, the rest of the group arrived on the early flight from London: Paul, John Sheridan, Mel and Len. John Sheridan was over to keep an eye on Tottenham's investment, as Lazio intended to check on the recovery of his knee. As soon as we had dumped our bags and had a quick bite to eat, we set off for the Olympic stadium. Once more there was an ecstatic welcome for Gazza and he responded to the love and adoration shown him. As usual in the derby matches, there was a lot of colour, noise and fireworks. The Roma fans had a large banner with the picture of a wheelchair on it for Gazza, while the Lazio contingent were a sea of blue and white flags. The stadium was nearly at bursting point with over 70,000 crammed into every available space. The match finished in a 1–1 draw, with Ruben Sosa scoring Lazio's goal. It was a typical result for a derby match;both sides were usually too frightened of losing to put on a convincing display. Rome was not a happy place for a beaten side, it wasn't unheard of for players from the losing team to stay home the following week and travel only to and from the training ground for fear of physical assaults and aggressive taunts from the public.

Gazza was pleased that his Dad had experienced a derby and they both agreed that it was incredible, like being in a kaleidoscope of ever-changing colours. Gazza still couldn't get used to the unquestioning hero worship from the fans, but he was enjoying it all, treating his fans like real human beings and happily signing autographs. As I was coming out of the hotel, I was stopped by an amazed Lazio fan.

'We can't believe it, he's like one of us. He talks and jokes with us. Most of the other players wouldn't give us the time of day, and they have not got half the talent that Gazza has. He is the star, and he talks to us.'

These were the fans that stood on the terraces week in and week out, who were used to seeing the players speed past them in their expensive cars after the match. Now here was a superstar, Gazza, willing to stop and have a chat. They loved him for it and that's one of the reasons why the normally impatient Italians were to be so understanding towards Gazza.

That evening we had a date with Telemontecarlo for their Sunday night sports show. There are three major football shows on Sunday night – 'Domenica Sportivo' on the state television, 'Pressing' on one of the private stations and 'Galagoal' on Telemontecarlo, plus a number of round-ups of the days events and highlights of goals from all the matches. It had been agreed that Gazza would appear on Galagoal after the derby for a five-figure sum.

Telemontecarlo had at that time a very glamorous presenter called Alba Parietti, who has since gone on to present the San Remo music festival and other important events. In this respect, Italy is very different to England. Where as an English sports programme wouldn't dream of having a glamorous female presenter, in Italy, no self-respecting sports programme would go on the air without a Miss Italy lookalike pouting for the camera. In England, it would be the equivalent of having Sharon Stone snuggled up between Saint and Greavsie, – a pretty disconcerting thought. Alba was, in fact, a highly intelligent woman and very good at her job, but she did tend to overdo things in her choice (or should I say, lack) of clothes. So we had to stifle our giggles as she came waltzing into the studio dressed in a tiny, fringed little black and silver number that was aimed at showing off her stunning legs. I observed Mick and the two John's sitting in the front row of the studio audience with their mouths open in utter disbelief. They obviously were not finding the show boring as they had previously thought!

Gazza had been given a red rose to present to Alba, which he did, albeit rather grudgingly. At the time, I put his sudden shyness at her presence down to being nervous in front of the camera, but on reflection and having since met Sheryl, he was probably terrified of pictures of him with glamorous Alba hitting the headlines. He soon started to relax though, and even enjoy himself. Walter Zenga, the Inter goalkeeper who also has a keen sense of humour, put Gazza at ease and had a bit of a laugh, taking the mickey out of the Englishman's collarless maroon suit and T-shirt.

'Who is your dress designer ... where do you buy your clothes?'

'From the local market stall, of course,' Gazza replied effortlessly, 'but when I'm on your money, I'll be able to afford something better.'

Even with one leg, Gazza retorted, he would be able to score against him. Zenga suggested they should have a contest whereby he would tie one arm behind his back and Gazza could shoot the ball at him. Unfortunately, it never happened but it would have been quite a laugh.

At the end of the show, there was a surprise in store for the audience, as on walked David Platt, in his first year with Italian club Bari, having just been made captain and enjoying every minute of his new status. The difference between the two English players was incredible. David had absorbed the Italian way of life with consummate ease. Dressed smartly in a navy Italian designer suit, he spoke the language, and was confident without being arrogant. One wondered if Gazza would undergo a similar transformation, particularly regarding the language, which was vital if he was to become fully intergrated into Italian football. As we all departed for the night, I briefly considered the fact that if Gazza had David Platt's character, then he wouldn't be Gazza, and we would miss out on his special talent. I suppose you just can't have everything in life.

On the Monday, Gazza had a checkup with the Lazio club doctor, Claudio Bartolini, which went very well. His rehabilitation was progressing smoothly and to plan. He had until 31 May 1992 to pass the fitness tests. Only then would he finally become a Lazio player.

That evening, we all paid a visit to the Rai television studios so that Gazza could appear on their 'Il Processo del Lunedi' show as specifically requested by Lazio. If Telemontecarlo was West Berlin, this was definitely East. We weren't told where to go or what to do, and nobody briefed us on what questions would be asked, as they had at Telemontecarlo. In fact, nobody seemed particularly concerned. Someone popped out and told us we would have to drive through the gates as though we were just arriving for the fans, who were lined up outside, and then we would be whisked into the studios, without, of course, being told where we were going to sit.Il Processo del Lunedi is presented by a man called Aldo Biscardi, who thinks he is wonderfully fair on everyone and runs a first-class show. Admittedly, it was not easy to co-ordinate as many things as he did on one show, and sometimes it did have its moments, but a lot of the time it was reduced to a gathering of screaming and shouting.

We dutifully 'arrived' for the fans and were then taken to the studio from where the show was coming out live. We located our seats only to find that the translation service wasn't working, so yours truly had to translate. After twenty minutes of discussing whether Van Basten should have been awarded a penalty or not, we made our excuses and escaped.

Tuesday was pancake day, or 'Fat Tuesday', in Italy. It was the day when all the 'fat' foods were used up before fasting, and in some countries, Italy being one, it was the day of Carnivale, when everyone had a party. We headed off downtown where crowds of youngsters were gathered. Gazza had a hat and glasses on and wasn't easily recognized. Unfortunately, an eagle-eyed police car had spotted our hero, and pulled up to request autographs, blocking the entire street. As if this wasn't enough, we then found ourselves being pelted with eggs by some boisterous Roma fans. At this point we decided, with 'minders' in tow, to head back to the hotel, whereupon Mick began organizing a sing-along session round the hotel piano.

There was a dinner going on, and at about eleven o'clock when the guests started to come out, they found Mick singing round the piano. They must have thought it was some kind of bizarre cabaret as within five minutes, Mick had them all singing and clapping along to 'Bye, bye blackbird' and 'When the saints come marching in'. Gazza completed the family atmosphere by going round with a collecting dish and making the equivalent of about £7, which he gave to the barman. Suddenly, a five-star hotel had become the Dunston, and everyone was enjoying themselves.

During the entire trip, Gazza had behaved impeccably. Unlike the August visit, he wasn't boozing or going to nightclubs with strange women. He was in bed by midnight every night, and up fresh in the morning the next day. It might have been the shock of the second injury, or some other influence, but it was definitely positive. In fact, after the second injury he had changed. Some of the bounce and joy had gone. Perhaps he felt that he had been betrayed by his people. To be attacked in his own city had left a deep scar of resentment, and he had subconsciously started to move away from his roots. Newcastle is a tough, hard town. Gazza had already experienced several run-ins during his time there from people who tried to bring him down a peg or two. Now they had started to make him question the very loyalty he always felt towards his home town. It made him all the more keen to get out to Italy and start a new life as soon as possible.

Gazza had a superstitious nature and felt sure that when he became established in Italy, his luck would change.

'I can't wait to get out here, Jane,' he would say, 'I can't wait to start playing again.'

He would soon get his wish. However, this growth away from his roots would become even more exaggerated in the months to come. For now it consisted of just a few cracks which could be papered over, but in time it would lead to conflict within his own family and circle of friends.

As May approached, things were beginning to hot up. It looked like Gazza was going to be fit, but one never knew until he actually passed the tests. Lazio had decided to come over and watch him play in a series of training matches, before everyone set off to Rome for the actual fitness tests. Lazio were paying a reputed £30,000 to bring top American knee surgeon, Jim Andrews over to Italy to give his opinion on the suspect knee.

The week beginning 18 May was crucial. The Lazio group flew over, headed by club doctor, Claudio Bartolini. Terry Venables, now firmly established as managing director of Tottenham Hotspur Football Club, was present to see how Gazza's knee would respond to all the twisting and turning in his first true test on the football pitch.

Gazza's first match took place at Mill Hill, Tottenham's training ground, in the pouring rain. It was Spurs' A-team against the reserves. Huddled under an umbrella was Dad John, who had come down from Newcastle to see his son take up the challenges of football again. Also lined up round the training pitch were an assortment of Italian and British journalists and television cameras. Confident that he would pass the fitness tests, Gazza joyfully got stuck in to the game and even scored a goal. At the end of the match, in typical Gazza style, he ran to the cameras and shouted, 'I'm back!' and then pitched himself headfirst into the nearest puddle.

Next day, the papers all carried reports of Gazza's first 'match' and that the deal now seemed likely to go through. Bartolini was satisfied with what he saw, and noticed no swelling in the knee when he examined it after the match. Next stop, Rome.

Lazio had lined up a series of tests to see how his knee had healed and to discover if there were any lingering problems from the operation. He was to have a full set of check-ups at the Institute of Scienza, and then examinations by Bartolini and Andrews followed by an MRI scan and an X-ray.

Like the final dramatic act of an opera, all the chief components in the Gazza saga, with the exception of Mel Stein, gathered in Rome. The first evening we all visited off to one of the nicest restaurants in town, Dal Bolognese in Piazza del Popolo, and horrified the owner by ordering a burnt steak with tomato ketchup for John Gascoigne. We had a table outside, but moved inside when Gazza said he didn't want photographs of him enjoying himself appearing in the papers when he was in Rome to prove his fitness. That was an extremely wise remark, prompted in part, no doubt, by the presence of the very attractive daughter of our hosts, whose presence Sheryl would not have appreciated.

Inside the restaurant, I had one of the biggest insights into Gazza's psychological state that I had ever experienced. As we all rearranged ourselves round the table, Gazza indicated that I should sit next to him. Once seated, he looked at me and without warning blurted out:

'I don't want it to get like before, with everyone always on at me. I can't take that kind of pressure, I hate it.'

'Paul, I'm here to take as much pressure off you as possible,' I replied.

'Don't let it get like before, Jane.'

'I won't, I promise.'

It was confirmation that he had not enjoyed the pressure put on him after the World Cup. At that moment, I felt very sorry for him. Here was a someone with a God-given talent, but without the inner confidence to handle it.

The next day, the fitness tests started at the Institute of Scienza near the Olympic Stadium. I followed Gazza round as he went into various rooms and was harnessed up to different machines. The first test was to see the functioning of his brain. He was wired up to what looked like a metal helmet with electrodes and then told to breathe normally and then deeply for several minutes to test how his brain responded to stress. The doctors then studied the printout to see if the peaks and troughs were normal – which surprisingly enough, they were!

On to the next machine, a scan, from which we watched his heartbeat. I was fascinated by the fact that you could see so clearly his heart valves opening and closing. John Sheridan was pacing about outside the room like an expectant father so I asked if he could be present. Having worked so closely with Gazza, he was naturally nervous about the results of the test. In fact, the only person who was calm was Gazza. He didn't seem to have any doubts as to whether he would pass the tests. There again, he knew his body better than anyone and if he felt good then he must have sensed his knee was completely healed. Besides, there had been so many medical people following him around that if anything had not healed properly the whole world would have known about it. On completion of the scan, his heart was pronounced as being stronger than most top athletes. No problem with his general fitness, then.

Next it was the bicycle, or the 'hamster wheel'. He was all wired up and off he went, pedalling madly while yards of paper spilled out of the machine with a record of his heartbeat, pulse, etc. All this time the journalists had been hanging around outside, their noses pressed to the glass window like over-enthusiastic bloodhounds. The bike test proved a success, and after a couple of chemical tests, urine and blood sampling, it was time to go. He had his photo taken with all the doctors and then we had an appointment with super surgeon, Jim Andrews.

Jim Andrews was an American doctor who specialized in treating injuries sustained by American footballs. He reckoned he could get a player back on the field within three to six months, but American football doesn't have the same demands, in terms of twisting and turning as European soccer does. We all went down to Lazio doctor Claudio Bartolini's hospital, San Giacomo in via Ripetta, in the centre of Rome. Like most state hospitals it was a bit of a wreck, with little attention paid to the decor, even though the medical care was very good. It seemed strange to have this visit taking place against a back-drop of bare walls and cheap furnishings. I suspected that Jim Andrews had Rembrandts on the walls of his clinic, whereas in Rome you were lucky to have paint on them.

Like a royal party, Jim Andrews swept down the main staircase surrounded by the professor of the hospital, several other specialists and Claudio Bartolini. We all squeezed into one of the examination rooms and Paul was introduced to Jim Andrews. He had to take his trousers off (it was then we discovered he didn't wear underpants) and lie on his stomach with his legs hanging over the edge of the examination couch. Andrews then looked to see if both legs were of equal height, which indicated if the knee was in good working order. Paul had to do a few standing jumps to see how his knee stood up. Then it was all over, and the doctors swept out of the room as quickly as they had entered.

Gianni Zeqireya took us back to the hotel, and it was rest time until the next round. I felt a bit like a circus trainer with a performing dog. Every now and then you would have to get it to jump through the hoops and stand on its hind legs clapping its paws together. Then everyone would say bravo and you could put it back in the kennel again, taking care it didn't bite your hand off.

On Saturday night, Gino Santin, who is an expert in these things, took us off to nearby Piazza Navona to enjoy a meal outside. All the doctors came along, as did actor Franco Nero, who had just returned from watching ex-wife Vanessa Redgrave perform in a play in London. There was quite an amusing exchange between Franco Nero and Gazza, when the Italian actor tried to explain the structure of the Latin and English languages, and point out how many similar words there were in each language. Gazza looked distinctly unconvinced.

Sunday was D-day. In the morning, Gazza had the MRI scan and the X-ray. For this, Lazio had arranged for the USI centre, which had all the latest equipment, to be open especially for us. Minder Gianni, John Sheridan, John Gascoigne, Gazza and I arrived and were taken through to wait in the reception room. It was a tranquil setting; the room had a balcony which overlooked a garden at the back of the building. After a few minute, we were escorted down to the scan room, where Gazza had to remove his watch, ring and credit cards before climbing on to the 'runway' and then being slid into the MRI machine. The poor chap had to lie still for nearly an hour while they took pictures. John Sheridan and I stood in the doorway and chatted to him to relieve the boredom.

John: 'You'll be back down the Dunston next week.'
Gazza: 'Hope I'll be a Lazio player as well.'
Jane: 'Maybe you'll turn into a Martian after all this.'
John: 'Maybe he already is.'

After a while the first results arrived and the negatives were put up on the screen to examine. John was interested, so I attempted to translate, which with a limited medical knowledge wasn't easy. The doctors were obviously studying them very carefully, and there seemed to be some discussion about several of them, which centred round a black spot clearly visible in the kneecap. I gathered that they were questioning whether the metal plate that had been placed in the kneecap when it was broken had damaged part of the cartilage, which was why there was a black spot. The atmosphere became tense. Was this a problem? Was he going to pass the fitness tests? The doctors refused to go into great detail, but they spent the next half hour going over and over the pictures which showed in great detail the inner workings of Gazza's knee. John and I looked at each other but were helpless to do anything. John is a very calm character and he thought it was highly unlikely that anything was wrong. Jim Andrews was due to arrive when we finished and they would obviously have to discuss their findings with him. Surgeon John Browett was also in Rome, so he could be involved in the discussion if necessary.

We moved onto the giant X-ray machine, which involved placing Gazza's right leg into the chamber with the other sticking straight up in the air outside it. The machine then moved the leg to various positions to get the best overall picture. The only problem was that it seemed to have a mind of its own, and became a kind of Chinese torture chamber. It took forty-five minutes to get it into place, by which time Gazza nearly had a muscle strain in his good leg, which was being pressed tightly up against the side of the machine. I could see he was starting to get agitated and was clearly uncomfortable. Fortunately, at the last minute, the machine decided to function normally, and the medical personnel managed to complete their task.

After another twenty minutes, we extracted him from the machine. As we were leaving, Jim Andrews was arriving fresh as a rose, with his entourage in tow, to study the results. Gazza hobbled out rubbing his good leg and we went off to get some lunch at the most exclusive riverside club in Rome, situated on the banks of the River Tiber. There we met up with Luca di Montezemolo, Chairman and Managing Director of Ferrari.

'Hi, how are you?' Luca greeted us.

'Nice to see you again,' replied Gazza. 'How's Ferrari?'

'Fine, come up and have a test drive.'

Gazza's eyes lit up at the thought of being behind the wheel of a Ferrari. 'Great, that'll be great,' he enthused in a broad Geordie accent, hardly able to contain his excitement. Ferraris just happen to be Paul's favourite cars.

We returned to our meal and Gazza was eager as ever, although his consumption of alcohol was noticeably light. He was being serious about the whole thing.

Lazio had decided to arrange a celebratory dinner that night for all the participants of this saga. Although they hadn't officially announced that everything was okay, this appeared to be an indication of their good intentions. However, as the time of the dinner neared, we all became less sure of the outcome.

The journalists were beginning to ask if everything was

alright as they had heard there was a last minute hiccup. Coming after what I had heard at USI, the whole thing began to worry us. It was a motley group that gathered on the terrace of the hospitality suite at the Eden Hotel for dinner that night. There was John and Penny Browett, the nice, well-behaved cultured guests of the piece. John Browett, the brilliant surgeon who had performed the vital operation on the patient, was alongside his attractive wife who also doubled up as his personal assistant. Then we had Terry Venables, who had worked his way up from the East End of London to become managing director of one of England's top football clubs, inspiring the love and devotion of the fans, and was like a second father to Gazza. John Sheridan was there, genuinely concerned about Gazza's welfare. John Gascoigne was looking proudly at his son, hoping it would all work out well in the end. Also in the group was the highly vocal American surgeon Jim Andrews, who was telling everyone about his valuable Ferrari collection. Then there was a cast of Italians who had assured us that they were going to spend a fortune on the patient and that he was going to live happily ever after with them. And last but not least, there was Gazza himself, pondering his fate. Would it be riches and further fame in a foreign land, or a retirement home in Newcastle?

We didn't have long to wait. As the Lazio managing director, Lionello Celon, stood up to make the toast, we all held our breath. Was he going to make the announcement now and clutch the player emotionally to his breast? No, he made a vague general speech welcoming us all to Rome, and then said he hoped it would all work out well. The tension was unbearable; the final fate of the player and maybe that of Tottenham Hotspur Football Club would not be known until tomorrow.

We had to go to the training ground for a few final tests on the pitch. Everyone was nervous and Gazza after a mozzarela breakfast, arrived at the Lazio training ground and made himself sick before he ran out onto the pitch to complete his fitness test. He repeated this action in front of the *Sun* photographer Richard Pelham a few months later. Once again, he was trying to keep his weight down. He had said in the car on the way to the ground, 'I shouldn't have eaten all that for breakfast, I'll have to get rid of it.'

The next day Terry Venables had a long meeting with Lazio, while the international press buzzed about upstairs. The idea was that an official announcement would be made the following day at Tottenham. But Lazio club doctor Claudio Bartolini seemed to pre-empt this when he announced: 'Now we have no doubts whatsoever. Tonight we fly to London and tomorrow we will tell the world that Gazza is part of Lazio. We have waited a year for this.'

It turned out that Terry's discussions with Lazio that morning had been about finalizing the deal and agreeing the arrangements for the two lucrative friendlies between Lazio and Spurs. I heard through Lazio that Mel and Len's fees for their work on the deal came to £400,000. This figure was also disclosed by Managing Director Lionello Celon in a conversation with a representative of Tottenham over dinner at the Hyde Park hotel in London.

On hearing confirmation of the deal, Jim Andrews said that Gazza was 'Superman' and went on proudly to say, 'You could say he's a lucky boy after two serious injuries to his knee. But he has proved his great spirit of competition which sets him apart from other athletes.'

John Sheridan admitted it was an 'emotional moment' for him, as he had to say goodbye to the boy he had grown so close to over the months of recuperation.

The superstar himself paid tribute to Terry Venables ('He made me a footballer. I listened to everything he said and learned. He's been fantastic. I owe him a lot. To me he's my second Dad') and also to John Browett and John Sheridan, without whom he wouldn't have been playing football again.

Terry hastily called a mini press conference and said how delighted he was that the deal had gone through, but he was also sad to see Gazza go. As he said to me while I was writing this book, 'It was a big disappointment when Gazza went, he's a big character, a gift and a real delight to have in a team. All the boys loved him. He could be a bit of trouble but he was well worth it.'

We all flew back to Heathrow where we were greeted by a line of clicking flashbulbs as we stepped off the plane, and by several television cameras on coming out of customs. Gazzamania was back. Having started in Italy during the 1990 World Cup, now two years later Gazza was set to become a star in the country that had provided him with an international stage for his talents. The next adventure was about to begin.

SHERYL AND PAUL

The week after we got back from Rome, Lionello Celon arrived to sign the final contract. Lazio had an end of season tournament in Canada and Brazil, and they wanted Gascoigne to meet up with the team in South America at the beginning of June. He wasn't too thrilled about this plan but agreed to go before he went on holiday with his family to Florida. We all had out inoculations, tetanus, cholera, typhoid etc, and felt ill for a day, then suddenly without warning the trip was cancelled by a phone call from Maurizio Manzini on the day we were due to depart. Then six hours later Lazio's lawyer Avvocato Mori turned up with the tickets, but it was too late by then, so I went to Rome to look for villas and apartments, and Gazza went on holiday.

The Gascoigne family departed en masse to Disney World in Florida, with their various partners. There was John and Carol, sister Anna with boyfriend John Paul, Paul with Sheryl, brother Carl went with Jimmy (even though they were not romantically involved!), and little sister Lindsay was accompanied by boyfriend Darren. Another couple of friends brought the number in the party to twelve. It was intended as Paul's farewell holiday for his family before he went to Italy. Unfortunately things didn't go quite as smoothly as planned, and there were arguments aplenty between Sheryl and the family. She spent a lot of the time shopping for jewellery, for which Paul usually picked up the tab. This involved thousands of pounds on, among other things, a gold and diamond ring which didn't go down too well with the others.

It was becoming increasingly obvious that Sheryl and Paul's family wouldn't be able to spend too much time together. Sheryl and Paul had also been having more arguments, and it seemed unlikely that she would come out to Italy in the summer to live with him.

It was important for Lazio and Paul that he had someone in Italy to keep him company. Brother Carl was coming out to take up the position that Glenn Roeder should have had, with an obvious difference that he wouldn't be involved in the technical side in any way, and wouldn't be able to build up the same kind of rapport with Lazio that Glenn would have done. As well as Carl, it was decided that Jimmy 'Five Bellies' would also come to live in Italy, the idea being that Carl and Jimmy would share an apartment and keep each other company.

At this stage I hadn't met either Carl or Jimmy, but their reputations had preceded them. I had heard all about Paul and Jimmy's escapades and fully expected a pair of complete yobs. On the day that Paul had signed the Lazio contract, he and Jimmy had amused themselves by shouting and screaming around the offices of Finers Solicitors and carried out such pranks as throwing cups of water from the balcony over the meeting rooms on unsuspecting solicitors below. It had got so bad that even Mel Stein had been forced to come out of the meeting and tell them to calm down. So I thought I would have my hands full with them all in Rome. In fact, it didn't end up like that at all.

I flew to Rome on the 6 July, one day before Gazza was due to arrive with his brother Carl, Jimmy, Mel and Len. We were all booked into the delightful Hotel degli Aranci and as soon as I'd arrived I checked the arrangements for the next day, and then decided to organize a surprise party for Mel Stein as it was soon to be his birthday. The Lazio marketing manager, Tommaso Cellini, had a friend who was involved in the horse show in Villa Borghese and we thought it would be a great idea to have the party there in the VIP centre.

The next day, I went to the airport with Mondiapol minders Gianni and Augusto. It was chaos, the fans were everywhere and there was an air of total hysteria. We went out on the tarmac to meet the plane with Maurizio Manzini, who was concerned about getting Paul through the wall of fans. The police weren't thrilled about it either, especially as they had to consider the safety of the other passengers, who were finding themselves in the middle of total pandemonium. I could just imagine a couple arranging to meet each other for a romantic weekend in Rome – 'See you at the airport, darling' – and then on arrival being surrounded by three thousand savages shouting

'Paul Gascoigne La La La La La,
Paul Gascoigne La La La La La.'

It was enough to put you off football and romantic holidays for life.

Gianni and Augusto worked a miracle and got us assembled by passport control. The first assault came from the journalists who were hungrily circling their prey just the other side of passport control, along with the television cameras and interviewers. It was decided that Carl, Jimmy and I would make our own way into town and leave the others to travel in the Mondiapol cars. That, at least, was the theory.

Carl, Jimmy and I picked up all the luggage and headed for customs, where we encountered total anarchy. At the same time that the police were forming a cordon to get Gazza through the crowd, a group of Japanese tourists were meandering through the airport. They were instructed to wait in the customs area, which naturally they did, in an orderly line, all with their matching luggage and Nikon cameras. Outside customs it sounded like the call of the wild and a few members of the Japanese contingent were starting to look rather alarmed.

The three of us walked through customs but Carl and Jimmy accidently led us into the Red channel, and we all promptly got stopped. Now Carl, Jimmy and Paul all had shaven heads at this time, which as one could imagine didn't exactly make them look like your average Joe Bloggs in the street. In fact, they more closely resembled a group of National Front activists, except one was being given a police escort through the airport, and the other two weren't. The customs man asked me where I'd come from, and when I replied Rome he was not amused. I had no documents to prove I'd been given permission to wander at will through the airport, and it looked like things were going to get nasty. I tried to find Maurizio or a policeman who I knew but they were all with Paul. I tried to explain to the customs man that the luggage belonged to that skinhead bloke being carted through customs by a dozen policemen but for some reason he didn't believe me, and he wanted us to open our luggage.

As the Gazza party hit the arrivals hall, the Lazio fans came surging forward and broke the police barriers. I suggested it might not be the right moment to ask Gazza for the keys to his luggage at the same time as the police were wading in with batons and two people were falling to the ground injured. I think the customs man got the message as after we'd managed to open a couple of cases he suddenly seemed to be in an awful hurry to have a tea break and so let us through. Throughout all this excitement, the Japanese group had been watching attentively, probably thinking it was some kind of strange Western summer ritual, and instead of the Colosseum, the place of passionate conflict was in actual fact Rome airport. As soon as a few bodies had been dragged to one side, the Japanese went on their way without a murmur to continue their tour of civilized Western countries.

There were a group of fans outside the hotel and a police car was parked outside to keep them all under control. We arrived in the hotel and after we had sorted out rooms and found our way round the place, we all gathered downstairs where the argument regarding dinner began.

Gazza's farewell party in Newcastle, with the presence of such honoured participants as Miss Whiplash, had been well chronicled in the press and Maurizio Manzini was very worried that Paul's presence at another party as soon as he hit Rome might give the fans the wrong impression. However, the party arranged at the horse show was intended to be very low key and just a celebration of Mel's birthday. As Paul was such an important part of Mel's life, it would have been a shame not to have him along. He was quite laid back about the whole thing and said he'd be happy to do whatever was best. The person who'd organized the dinner was desperate to have Paul, not for the publicity, but because he'd promised his colleagues that Gazza would be along and didn't want to lose face in front of them.

After half an hour of arguing, I took control of the situation, went over to Paul and said, 'Look why don't you come along for an hour, then go back to the hotel. That way no-one can say you were out half the night, and everyone will be happy.' He agreed. Maurizio was still unhappy and was seen going off into the night hanging on to the back of Cellini's moped with his mobile telephone talking to the Lazio hierarchy and explaining the whole thing was nothing to do with him. I didn't mind taking responsibility as I was pretty sure that everything was well organized. Tiziana Maestrelli and I had made a trip out to the site to check there weren't hordes of journalists present. The area where we were to sit for dinner was cut off from the rest and as private as possible. So it was all systems go.

We arrived and were given a king's welcome by the workers, then seated at a long table which was festooned in blue and white ribbons. Once we'd established what Mel and Len could and couldn't eat, we were ready to tuck in. We had a delicious pasta, followed by meat and then fruit and the cake, which for festive purposes was definitely made with vegetable fat! Gianni and Augusto were with us, plus the group from England and a couple of my friends Tiziana and Sabrina, another ex- Italia '90 person. After the meal we went for a wander around the show and took a look at the 'calcetto' (five-a-side) football, which was being played under flood-lights. Proceedings were brought to a halt as Gazza appeared and all the players rushed up to say hello. It was another demonstration of how everyone was attracted to him. Gazza was very relaxed and in good humour. Once again he was back in a country which was full of people who were on his side. There wasn't anyone who wanted to pull him down and he felt very secure.

At eleven o'clock several journalists were seen by the entrance to the VIP village, so I suggested to Gazza that he return to the hotel. Without a word of protest he departed, and everyone was happy. We stayed for a while then went back to the hotel, where there were about twenty or thirty fans wandering about or standing with their noses glued to the gates, in case their superstar appeared.

The next day we went down to the local banks with the idea of opening accounts for Paul. One would receive Paul's monthly wages, while the other would hold his current account. We turned up with a police car full of uniformed police, an unmarked police car, Augusto with Paul in the armoured Mercedes, the Chrysalis television crew plus assorted journalists. A rather over the top way, I thought, of impressing the bank manager!

The next day, Mel and Len returned to London, and we started looking for villas. This wasn't easy, first because most of the estate agencies are closed in July and August, and second because Gazza didn't want anything that wasn't absolutely private. He really wanted the villa we had seen last year, but in the meantime it had been sold and so it just wasn't possible to have it. I tried to extract from him what sort of villa he wanted. 'One with a swimming pool and a garden. And it must be private,' was Gazza's reply. Len Lazarus had also specified the maximum amount that could be spent. The problem was, the villas Paul liked were the ones costing up to fifteen million lire a month, a figure that Len said was out of the question. This led to a confrontation with Len as Paul was getting more and more frustrated. After we'd seen one pretty villa with a tiny garden, Paul confided in me.

'You wouldn't fit a bloody jacuzzi in here, let alone a swimming pool. Why are we looking at places like this?'

'Because they're within your price range,' I said, 'and Len says you can't spend any more.'

'But its my money,' he said defensively.

'I know, but I'm stuck in the middle between what you want and what Len's telling me I can spend.' I paused.

'I'll have a word with Len. It's not fair on you, you're trying your best,' he replied.

After a week of searching at the upper end of the market, I was beginning to panic. We had almost exhausted the supply of villas in the northern outskirts of Rome and had yet to find a suitable one. The pressure was on as Paul was insisting he wanted to move in when he came back from training camp on 10 August.

The first few weeks had been incredible, not least because Gazza, although he was desperate to find a home, seemed to be genuinely pleased and excited to be in Italy. The fans loved him, and he was inspired by them to write another poem, which he wrote down in my notebook – this time about Lazio's derby match against AS Roma.

Blue is the colour
Lazio is the name
I am the other
Football is the game

When we are together
We will be the best
We will take on Rome
and the f---ing rest

The we'll take on Juve
Sampdoria, Napoli too
We will shit on all of them
Especially that Roma crew

Now never mind the league
Or the bastard cup
Because when we play the derby
We will f--- them up.

It seemed as if the injury and the bad times in England were finally behind him. He thought that all he had to do was train hard and he would be playing his first match with Lazio as the season began. However, things weren't going to work out quite like that.

Life in Rome wasn't turning out to be just an extended holiday for Gazza. Lazio were not happy at what had come back from America, so he was taken to the IMS for tests and then put on a diet. If they expected to get a reasonably in-condition football player, they were to be sadly disappointed. He was overweight and unfit, more suited to playing chess than football.

The press had all made a big thing of his weight problem. In fact, according to Lazio doctor Claudio Bartolini, he was then only 4 kg over his ideal weight of 78 kg. His general fitness, however, wasn't great. The medical report stated that the muscular content of his body had to a great part been substituted by 'adipose mass', that is, fat especially on the trunk and abdominal areas. He also had a bit of colic gastritis and a slight case of pharyngitis.

The weight problem was not unknown to Tottenham, and when he had come back overweight from a holiday once, Terry Venables had to put him on a strict diet, which had resulted in him losing weight very quickly. But with this weight loss came a loss of strength, and he couldn't last ninety minutes on the pitch, so a gradual reduction in weight was recommended the next time round.

The Lazio medical team commented that Gazza's way of eating was disorderly, incorrect and unbalanced. The haphazard intake of Chinese takeaways, hamburgers and chips was not appreciated in a country which took its diet very seriously. So they gave him a fitness programme and put him on a diet.

The fitness programme was due to take place during the period 9–16 July, when the team was at Norcia training together. Lazio hoped that a typical day in the life of Paul Gascoigne would look as follows:

8.00 am Wake up call
9.00 am To the training ground
1.00 pm Lunch
2.00 pm Afternoon rest!
5.00 pm To the training ground or to the Institute of Medicine and Sport to do various supervised exercises
8.00 pm Dinner
11.30 pm Sleep (at least 8 hours!)

The diet was à laugh. I read it to him as we were driving along to the clinic.

'What do you fancy for lunch, Gazza? Grated celery or pureed carrot? With lemon dressing, of course, no oil.'

He pulled a face.

'Then you can have 80 g of normal pasta or 100 g of wholemeal pasta with tomato sauce, and a teaspoon of parmesan cheese.'

'Hmm,' he grunted unenthusiastically.

'Breakfast is a real feast. A couple of wholemeal biscuits with a scrap of jam and honey, and a cup of tea ...'

By this time all of us, including the driver Augusto, were in hysterics over the prospect of witnessing Gazza tucking in to all this yummy food.

Italian players were used to having dietary considerations as part of their training programme, and Claudio Bartolini was determined to see a slimmer, fitter Gascoigne. His team-mates, Riedle and Doll had both profited from the Italian diet and turned into streamlined versions of their former selves. Gazza, however, was used to a high level of carbohydrates and it would be difficult to wean him off Big Macs and onto apples and pears.

Jimmy decided to keep him company. Fed up with the nickname 'Five Bellies' ('... the worst thing Paul's ever done to me') he decided to lose weight. Rather than take things gradually, he decided to take drastic action, and not only stop eating anything except salads, but start running up and down the hill outside the hotel every afternoon in the steaming heat. I told him he'd kill himself, but he was too intent on getting a lithe body. In fact, what did happen was that his stomach went into rebellion, having had fast food chucked into it for the last twenty-six or so years, and everything just went straight through him, or sometimes came up again. As if that wasn't enough, Carl had an ulcer and was feeling ill most of the time, suffering from fainting spells and an upset stomach. So, I was keeping an eye on both of them to make sure they didn't end up in hospital. In the meantime, I had to find a flat for Jimmy and Carl.

There were quite a few press blokes about the place, and I tried to keep up a PR job, and let Paul pose for photos or talk to journalists if he felt like doing so. Paul Callan of the *Daily Express* was in Rome and asked for a photo of himself with Paul, which he then made into an article which seemed as though they'd had dinner together. It was, however, quite harmless and showed that Paul was settling down well. Mel was not quite so pleased. When he saw the article he was cross as he reckoned they had got a free exclusive.

Mark Palmer from the *Sunday Telegraph* was also in Rome and he accompanied Carl, Jimmy and I on a flat hunt. We were all driving along in the taxi when Mark and I through general conversation discovered that we were distant cousins. Jimmy, with typical dry northern humour, commented, 'You'll be husband and wife next'. It was a good time for press relations. Gazza was more relaxed than I've ever seen him with the journalists.

We had a good laugh during the first few weeks. There were a group of spectacular transvestites who inhabited the area round the Flaminia stadium and we used to drive round with Gazza hanging out of the car window yelling insults at them, such as 'frocio', which means gay. 'Look, look, incredible, that's a guy, he's got balls,' as we passed one with nothing on but a pair of tango briefs. 'Look at that one!' he'd say as we passed another, a stunning blonde. The transvestites were quite amazing, all men but with bodies like beautiful women and huge chests. It became an after-dinner habit to drive round to see them, with the unmarked police car in tow! Once, to disguise himself Gazza wrapped loo roll round his head to look like a mummy and stuck a cigar in his mouth. Lazio had bought a young Brazilian player and one night, feeling sorry for him as he was always in the hotel, we dragged him out to Piazza Navona and then sent him down to see the transvestites with Jimmy in the Panda. They were thrilled to see one of their own, most of them being Latin American, and they all wanted to get into the car. On seeing this, Jimmy put his foot down hard on the accelerator and drove off pretty quickly!

A few days before Lazio took off to start their pre-season training, Aron Winter turned up at the Hotel degli Aranci with his girlfriend, Yvonne. Bought by Lazio to provide cover for Gascoigne in case he took a while to get back into playing regular first-team football, Aron was to turn into the club's best buy of the year. A tranquil, well mannered lad, he was easy going and fitted in anywhere with few problems. I think he was surprised to confront so many crazy Geordies in one place, and wondered what he had got himself into, but he seemed very positive about being in Italy, and most importantly he lacked the arrogance of most of the other new boys. Gazza made him feel at home by turning up at his hotel room wearing nothing but a pair of sunglasses. Aron appreciated a laugh although, like many, he sometimes found Gazza's jokes a bit over the top, especially some of the dressing room tricks.

The team set off for Norcia , while I stayed back in Rome to look for villas, sort things out and also prepare for Sheryl's visit. Sheryl was due out on the 19 July, a couple of days before Paul was to return from Norcia. The idea was that she would look at the villas I'd found and then Paul would look at them to decide which one they would take. They had obviously made up after the fights in Florida and now she was going to come out and live with him in Italy. I have no idea who made the first move to re-establish relations, but she was one of several people who had sent him a card to wish him luck in his Italian adventure and say how much she and Mason would miss him.

Paul rang me to say Sheryl was coming.

'That will be nice,' I said.

'She's a nice lass,' he continued, 'had a hard time, but she's a nice girl.'

Paul was never particularly forthcoming about his women, apart from going into details about their sexual prowess to his mates. From the way he talked about Sheryl, she scored a straight 10 out of 10 every time. Even Gianni Zeqireya was surprised by some of the more 'creative' activities.

I had spoken to her a couple of times before she came out to Italy, and she sounded quite pleasant and very independent. She had said she didn't want to put me to any trouble and assured me she could look after herself. So I got a taxi and went to meet her at the airport.

Having seen pictures of Sheryl, I knew that I should expect a very glamorous blonde, and I recognized her as soon as she came through customs. She was with her mum, with Mason balanced on the luggage trolley. We greeted each other and all set off to the Hilton, where she was staying. Sheryl was someone who liked luxury, and she had decided that the three-star Hotel degli Aranci, however friendly, wasn't going to be quite to her taste. To be fair, with a small child she probably wanted a swimming pool to ease the effect of the heat.

I can remember that I thought she seemed quite nice. She was very different from the local girls in Newcastle and I thought this would have advantages and disadvantages. Paul was now moving in different circles to those he'd been brought up in, and he needed someone who could cope with the new life style, while at the same time understanding that he was still a Geordie boy at heart. It was a very tricky problem for anyone to negotiate.

A friend of Paul's, Marco Dolfus, had very kindly lent me a Mini so I could get around Rome. So for the next couple of days, Sheryl and I drove about the countryside looking for villas in the searing heat. During this time she left Mason with her mother in the hotel, and they swam or played in the shade.

As we were driving round, Sheryl talked to me about her broken marriage and how her husband had not been paying her any maintenance money, and how good Paul had been and how much he adored Mason.

'My marriage was over before I met Paul,' she said. 'We were living apart even if we did share the same house. Then Colin moved out.

'Paul and I were just good friends for a long time. You know he saw other women and I saw other men.' She added hastily, '... although I didn't sleep with anyone else, of course.'

Sheryl was very defensive as to her daughter Bianca's decision to live with her father: 'You can imagine how upset I was, I'm her mother. But if that's what she wants then its better for her.' Sheryl was a strong, dominant person who was used to being the centre of attention, having been brought up as an only child, although she had two step-brothers. Not having the economic means to bring up her two sons, her mother Susan had let her sons go to live with their father, and this was to have an enormous influence on Sheryl's own attitude towards her ex-husband's desire to see his children. Sheryl was very much of the opinion that once a marriage was over you cut all the bonds and got on with your own life. The fact that she'd allowed Mason to think that Paul was his father, was a way of closing one chapter of her life and getting on with the rest. But as a young mother struggling to bring up two kids on her own, I did feel sorry for her.

It seemed that Sheryl had been indulged as a child, especially by her grandparents, who adored her. She'd suddenly woken up to the fact when an early boyfriend had cheated on her. They had been going out since they were fourteen.

'I came home one night,' she said, 'and for some strange reason I drove past my house and down the road. My boyfriend's car was parked in an unusual place, and at that moment I just knew he was with another girl. I went home and kept ringing until he answered. Then he came round and confessed. He'd been making love to someone else.'

The hapless boyfriend was given his marching orders and I think this incident had an effect on Sheryl's entire view of both men and women. During her marriage, she was eventually transformed from a sweet, good looking, quite prim lady (she considered anyone who had streaks in her hair was a 'slagbag') into a super-glamorous dolly bird set on getting what she wanted out of life.

Certainly, it seemed at this stage as if her relationship with Paul was going full steam ahead. He obviously adored her and was desperate to have her in Rome with him. At the time I thought she would be good for him, as being insecure he needed someone who would give him a stable base, and was strong and loving. The only problem, which I didn't realize at the time was Sheryl's dislike of football and her need for the company of her family and friends, both things which would eventually lead to her return to England.

But in the early days it seemed as if she was prepared to move out to be with Paul and share her life with him. They had effectively been living together in England, and as each had their own circle of friends, it had worked very well. If Paul hadn't invited her to live with him in Italy, she would have gone to America to live near her step-brothers, and so frightened by the thought of losing her, he had taken the step of getting her to come and live in Italy. At the time, Lazio were more than happy with the decision as they felt that footballers settled down better in a foreign country if they had a happy and stable home life.

The day after Sheryl arrived in Rome, Carl got on a flight back to Newcastle to cure his ulcer problems. For Jimmy this was obviously quite difficult as he was now on his own in a foreign country, in which he didn't speak the language and in the middle of summer when a lot of places, including shops were closed. Meanwhile, Paul was having a baptism of fire with the team in Norcia. As Umbria isn't very far from Rome, there were hundreds of fans who decided to make the journey and go and visit their heroes. This resulted in chaos as the hotel did not have adequate security. One day Gazza and his room-mate, Claudio Sclosa, were astounded to find a fan climbing through the window of their room. Sclosa had to grab him by the neck and throw him out. Fortunately for Gazza, Claudio Sclosa was an easy going, level-headed sort of person who would always try, without much success, to steer Gazza along the right lines and encourage him to learn the language.

On 21 July, Lazio returned to Rome, and Paul disappeared straight to the Hilton to see Sheryl and Mason. He had three days off before the team were to go up to their summer training camp at Seefeld in Austria.

We did manage to look at a villa which Paul decided to take. I was beginning to wonder if he was ever going to find one that fitted his high expectations, but at last one materialized. Situated on the via Guistiniana, it was totally private, being reached by a small slip road, off the main road. The house was behind electronic gates with a high wall on either side. Inside the grounds stretched round both sides of the house, with an orchard and a swimming pool. The actual house was on three levels and had four bedrooms and four bathrooms. There was a billiard table, built of mahogany with intricate brass (I presume they weren't gold!) decorations, which once belonged to the ex-king of Italy. The current owner, Mario Quattrocchi, wanted to rent it out for a year, for the astronomical sum of 15 million lire a month, which worked out at nearly £7,500. But it was the only villa that Gazza had seen that he really liked apart from the one the previous year. The villa had a desert camper in the garden, complete with air conditioning and comfortable sleeping quarters. There weren't many away matches planned for the desert, but we were sure it would come in handy one day when Lazio played a friendly in Africa, perhaps. There was also a Range Rover and mountain cross country motorbike.

At first the owner insisted on an outrageous amount of money as a deposit, nearly a year or something similar. We said no, but we'd provide a letter of credit for three month's rent, which could act as a deposit. But Quattrocchi didn't want this, which is when we all got a bit worried about the situation. Mel Stein wasn't too happy, but he was under pressure from Paul to sort out the villa, so we agreed to pay no deposit, but provide a year's rent in advance.

On the 24 July, Lazio headed off to the cool mountain air, and the next day I went to the Hilton and had a drink with Sheryl. I was also trying to keep Jimmy's spirits up, as he was feeling a bit down about the fact that Paul hadn't contacted him in the three days that he had off from training. But this was to be a recurring theme. On the 26 July, Jimmy's girlfriend, Anna and his son Liam, arrived in Rome with a friend to visit him, and he moved into his apartment. We had to check out of the Hotel degli Aranci, and I sent the hotel bill, which had thousands of pounds of telephone calls and a huge bar bill, to Lazio, who were to pay for accommodation. Sheryl also left that day, and I had to pack Paul's clothes and take them to Jimmy's apartment. He had brought everything: winter clothes, leather jackets, tennis rackets, the lot and at eleven o'clock at night a friend and I were packing them into suitcases to take them round to Jimmy's flat.

By the time I got home, I was exhausted. First thing next morning, the phone rang. It was Paul from Austria, asking me if I had mentioned girls to Sheryl. I was half asleep at the time, but there was clearly something wrong. This wouldn't be the first or the last time.

I flew home for a week on 1 August, as my mother was ill in hospital. By the time I got back a week later, Sheryl had returned with Mason. She had sent all her furniture and various possessions along with Paul's, by road. Everything was due to arrive in the next few days.

Paul needed a car while we were negotiating with a company to get him one free in exchange for publicity, so I arranged for the hire of a Mercedes for him. I went and collected Paul from the training ground when the team arrived back from Seefeld, and he drove us back to the Hilton. On our arrival, I was climbing out of the car when suddenly Paul leapt out and dashed off to another vehicle that was parked behind us. He paused by the driver's door and promptly started yelling and shouting at the occupants, even grabbing one by the throat. I saw they had cameras and my heart sank. I thought they were probably American tourists who were taking snapshots of their happy holiday hotel, only to be upset by some incoherent Geordie lout jumping up and down and screaming at them. I dashed over and suggested to Paul that he go inside the hotel.

It was then established that the people in the car were, in fact, photographers and I called the Hilton security people, who came and gave them a dressing down. I explained who I was and asked them to contact me if they should want to take photos, rather than just head off and invade Paul's privacy. I thought that if we gave them maybe one at-home shot, or one holiday shot, they would disappear and not bother Paul again. Perhaps this was naive of me, but I thought it was better to try and establish lines of communication rather than let the paparazzi just run loose. But when I explained this to Mel, it fell on deaf ears. Who knows which one of us would have been right? Certainly, the same photographers had already caused Paul several problems, lying in wait outside his house, where they had taken pictures of Sheryl topless, and following him to restaurants. If there was one thing that irritated Paul above all else, it was invasion of privacy.

The next day, Paul moved into the villa with Sheryl and Mason. I had to dash over to the shipper to give them the translation of the list of goods that was to arrive the next day from England. I got a bit stuck on 'large hippo toy' and 'toy oven', but apart from that things weren't too difficult. I also had to leave a million lire as deposit in customs as Paul hadn't yet obtained his resident certificate, so couldn't prove he was living in Rome.

The day after, the lorry arrived and Paul, Sheryl, Jimmy and I unpacked 80 boxes of things! The owner had left his animals behind and so Paul inherited an Alsatian dog and her puppies, along with a black cat. Only Paul could rent a house in which there was a ready-made Noah's Ark. Being superstitious, Paul was freaked out about the black cat, but I hoped he would settle down and let them all stay.

Mel and Len arrived that night and stayed at the villa. They had come over for meetings with the bank and with Lazio. At eleven o'clock, I left them all to it and went home to sleep. I was beginning to realize that this was going to be a 24-hour-a-day job, seven days a week.

The next couple of days were fairly difficult as the hot water kept going off upstairs, which meant everyone had to have cold showers, but that was eventually sorted out, and the mechanics of the villa seemed to settle down.

On 17 August, Graham Taylor arrived in Rome. He had been in contact with me previously to arrange when it would be a good time to come to visit Lazio. Taylor was very keen on building up good relations with all the clubs that had England players, and he decided to come to Italy to visit Lazio, Juventus and Sampdoria. Bearing in mind Gascoigne's injury and his long lay-off period, Graham was particularly keen to ensure that things went well between himself and Lazio. He knew that he would have to rely on the Lazio to advise him when Gazza would be ready to play again, and he felt it was a good idea to hold out the olive branch and show that the English FA was keen to be in close contact with the Italian club. Lazio very much appreciated this, as they were used to being informed as to when a national team required its players and then not see the managers from one month to the next. They liked Taylor's open, honest approach and were happy to discuss things with him. The rapport between the Italian club and the England manager was immediate and very positive.

Another reason for his visit was to allow him to get close to Gascoigne. Graham Taylor hadn't had a lot of time with his star player. He didn't play him in the England–Republic of Ireland game, and he hadn't seen much of him before he had been out through injury, first the hernia and then the knee. Graham knew that Gascoigne was going to be an important part of the qualifying matches for the 1994 World Cup. He also thought it was important to try and get inside Gazza's head and understand what made him tick, so he could make the most of him, and give him encouragement and support when necessary.

I tried to leave the two of them alone together as often as possible, so they could start sorting things out. We all had a meeting with Gascoigne and the Lazio management before Lazio's friendly match against a Brazilian team in the Olympic stadium. Managing director, Lionello Celon was present, along with doctor Claudio Bartolini, coach Dino Zoff and team manager Maurizio Manzini. As long as the player was fit, the club were obliged, under UEFA rules, to release him for a maximum of seven international matches. The penalty for not complying to these rules was a fine of 200,000 Swiss francs. It has been known for clubs to pay this rather than release their star player if they had an important league match to play. Taylor had seven qualifying matches to come and a friendly in Spain in a couple of weeks time. He wanted to take Gazza with him to Spain to allow him to get used to being back in the England set-up. The England manager knew that it was unlikely that Gazza would have played a club match by this time, and therefore unlikely that Lazio would release him to play, but he wanted him to be a part of the England squad. He needed Lazio to agree that Gazza could go to Spain and then also be released for the seven matches, two of which would mean he would miss a couple of Serie A matches at the end of the season.

Taylor put his case forward. 'I would be willing to cooperate in any way possible with the club. If you would like to send the team doctor out to Spain to monitor his progress, then we would be happy to accommodate him.'

The Lazio management understood the importance of Gazza's presence in the England squad after such a long absence, from the point of view of team spirit if nothing else, and they agreed that Gazza could go on the understanding that if he had not played in the league, he would not play for England.

It was an extremely cordial meeting, with both sides understanding the other and quickly reaching agreement. Dino Zoff is a man of few words, but having been captain of the national team and having won the World Cup in 1982, he understood more than most the needs of a national team manager. As far as Gazza was concerned, he was absolutely dying to get back in the national team. He wasn't being allowed to play football with Lazio, who were being cautious in his rehabilitation programme, so he was feeling a little frustrated and was eager to get back into the fray.

Graham Taylor attended the Lazio training session on 18

August to see how Gazza was getting on. Gazza trained with the rest of the team, but held back on using full force when kicking the ball. After the session, he confessed to Graham that he had pulled a thigh muscle. It was then Graham's difficult job to inform Lazio, who were less than happy about hearing the news from anyone other than the player. But that was typical of Paul, he badly wanted to play again and he thought that if he didn't talk about the injury, it would just go away. (He had picked up a similar injury while playing for Newcastle in a match against Nottingham Forest. He had hidden it from Dave Sexton on being called into the England Under-21 side, and went on to have a terrible match.) This type of thigh strain was not unusual in a player struggling to get back to full fitness after a long layoff, but Paul was nevertheless disappointed as he thought that once he was declared fit in May, it would be easy to get back to full fitness. Now he was laid off training to undergo ten days of massage and physiotherapy.

In spite of all this, Graham Taylor left Italy in a more contented frame of mind. Although Paul had picked up another injury, it had been minor one and Graham had a major breakthrough in his relationship with Paul. They had a good chat and Paul had shown respect and confidence in his national team manager.

On 19 August, I went back home for ten days to see my mother who was now out of hospital and recovering. I left Paul and Sheryl happily settling in to the villa, and presumed they would still be happy when I returned.

I arrived back on 30 August with my car and all my luggage. I then tried to phone the villa. There was no answer, so I thought they had probably gone out for the day. Later I tried again and again, but no answer. The weather was pretty unsettled with the odd thunderstorm, so I thought it was strange there was nobody about. By ten o'clock, I was getting worried. It was unlikely that they weren't the house, or at least that someone wasn't in the house, as Mason would be in bed.

I rang Gianni Zeqireya, and he said he would go round and investigate. I then phoned the owner and arranged to meet him the next day to sort out the water problems.

The next morning, there still no reply from the villa, and by now I was getting very worried. I drove to the house and met the owner who was waiting outside the gates, which were wide open. At this point I was panicking, as I thought Gazza had been kidnapped and was at this moment lying tied up in the boot of some kidnapper's car heading down to Aspromonte – kidnap country. With some trepidation, I approached the villa and found Gazza's Mercedes in the drive. I knocked on the door of the house, to be greeted by Sheryl with a broom in her hands. I said that I hadn't been able to get hold of them, and she explained that the thunderstorm had knocked out the telephone. I asked where Paul was, and she said he was at the training ground. I wondered how he had got there, as the car was in the drive. She explained that the car wasn't working as it had a flat battery, so he had taken the mountain motorbike. They had an argument so they weren't speaking. Sheryl was rather quiet and withdrawn and things had obviously gone downhill since I left them ten days ago. Bianca was now with them, as well as Mason. Apparently, she had been missing her mother and wanted to come to Rome, so Paul had agreed, although he had a closer relationship with Mason, who called him Daddy.

My first worry was that Paul was on a motorbike with no insurance and no crash helmet and a knee which, if he fell off, could be wrecked forever. I rang the training ground and they said that he had arrived safely. Fortunately, Maurizio Manzini wasn't at the ground or he would have had a heart attack seeing his star purchase, the player it had taken fifteen months of hard negotiation to buy, arrive on a motorbike.

I asked the people at the training ground to hang on to Paul and I would come and fetch him, but he decided to make his own way back, and after training turned up with Gianni Zeqireya and the motorbike in the boot of the car. Apparently, the back wheel had stuck whilst Gazza was doing 100 km/h, and Gianni had come along and rescued him. As soon as he got out of the car, I could see that Gazza was agitated.

'I've got a few problems,' he said. 'Sheryl needs a car so she's not stuck in the house all day, and she needs a babysitter so we can go out sometimes.'

There were also certain things that weren't working, like the hot water and the electronic gates. He also wanted the owner's furniture stored, as the house was full of furniture, and the dogs removed if at all possible. The bitch was barking all night and keeping him awake. He had partly resolved this problem by having a stroke of brilliance one night as the dog was barking under his bedroom window at two in the morning. He had tried screaming every swear word in the book at her with no result. Finally, he decided he would try it in Italian, so he grabbed the dictionary and looked up two words, then opened the window and screamed, 'Silenzio, bastardo'. It had worked and the dog shut up.

I immediately arranged a car for Sheryl, but the babysitter was slightly more complicated as you couldn't just have any person in the villa, and so I started to ask around at Lazio and with people I knew.

Meanwhile, Chrysalis were waiting to start recording the interviews and other material for the Channel Four Saturday programme featuring Paul. Gazza agreed to meet them at the Hilton at 3 pm, then I would take Sheryl off to pick up the car and she would drive home. I went off to the Hilton and met the Chrysalis crew. Three o'clock came and went, and at 3.15, I decided to ring the villa. Sheryl answered, and when I asked where Paul was, she said he had been trying to get me. He had gone off with Gianni, and she was going home. I presumed she meant for a few days, which as they were arguing seemed a good idea, as maybe they would get their problems sorted out and she would come back with a new view on things. But no, she said she was leaving for good. I asked her to wait until I got over to the villa, she said there was a taxi coming at 4 pm.

As it was now 3.20, I got into the car and dashed over. I dropped Neil Duncanson off at the training ground, so he could wait for Paul who was due to train later that afternoon.

When I got to the villa, I found Sheryl packing cases in the bedroom and the kids gathering up their toys. She explained that she had had enough and she couldn't stand Paul's behaviour anymore. She always had to do what he wanted to do all the time and they were always fighting. On one occasion, Paul had pinned her against the wall and screamed at her, telling her he didn't think she was the greatest woman in the world. Sheryl felt she couldn't do what she wanted to do. She was upset, as were the children.

I tried to get her to stay by pointing out that it was early days, and they were settling into a new country, and she shouldn't just throw everything away before giving it a go. She was adamant, however, that she was going. The taxi arrived, and she swiftly climbed in with the children and set off. The kids had been concerned by all this, and Bianca had enquired, in a somewhat resigned fashion, where their next house would be.

I phoned Paul at the training ground.

'What did she say?' he asked me.

'That she's fed up with you.'

'Look, I've phoned Anna and John and they're coming out tonight. Can you organize the tickets?' He gave me his credit card details.

'I feel sorry for the kids,' I ventured

'I know, come to the training ground.'

At the training ground I found Chrysalis wondering if they were going to get any filming done, and Paul in a bit of a state. I sat him down and we had a chat.

'I've got a lot of problems at the moment. Me money's not going into the bank, the water keeps going off, the dog's barking (again). It's getting me down.' He was extremely agitated, biting his fingernails and spitting on the ground.

'We can sort out the bank,' I said. 'Lazio made a big mistake in sending instructions to the bank by letter (which they had). I'll call the owner of the villa and sort out the problems.'

I felt sorry for him, as I could understand that moving jobs to a foreign country was very difficult, but doubly so if you were a footballer and had been used to having everything done for you, and only had to worry about tying up your boot-laces. Terry Venables had been excellent in dealing with this and had always made sure Paul didn't have things worrying him off the pitch.

But Italian clubs were a little different. In Italy playing football was a highly professional, highly commercial enterprise and they were not as soft or human as the English clubs, although it must be said that Lazio were a lot more understanding than most. Juventus, for example, had alienated Ian Rush by not giving him the necessary support. Ian had been left to find his own villa when he returned from summer training, which had taken, him, me and a friendly Italian journalist an afternoon to locate. It took them a few months to sort out two cars for him, so when wife Tracey had to attend early morning Italian lessons, he was getting up at the crack of dawn to take her to the school, and was therefore too tired to train! Juventus had also demonstrated they knew little about psychology by calling Ian in to tell him off for not signing an autograph for a fan, without complimenting him on the fact that he was scoring in every pre-season friendly. Lazio, fortunately for Gazza, were much more considerate about their investment. They were totally committed to Gazza, and in the following months they were to demonstrate both understanding and sensitivity in dealing with him.

Gazza decided to let things lie for a few days, so we didn't cancel the school places that we booked for Bianca and Mason. Chrysalis managed to do a couple of photos with the presenters of the programme, then we all went to La Campagnola, a restaurant near the training ground. We sat down at a table next to Giorgio Chinaglia, ex *enfant terrible* of Lazio. Chinaglia had been the star striker of Lazio's 1974 league championship winning team and had later gone on to play for Cosmos in the States. He had also been a great character and an exceptional talent and, like Gazza, had problems in keeping his exuberant character in control.

Feeling depressed Gazza started to drink heavily, and by the time Gianni and I left to go to the airport to pick up Anna and John, the empty bottles were beginning to line up.

The plane was on time and we found Anna and John waiting for us just outside the airport building. Anna and Paul are like twins, both to look at and to a certain extent in personality, except that Anna was stronger in character, just like her mum. She was as talented as her younger brother, being a great singer and a very promising actress. Living in the shadow of Paul hadn't always been easy, but Anna had the drive and ambition to make sure people took her for what she was and not because of her famous relation.

By the time we got back to the restaurant, Paul was well and truly away, he had been drinking champagne and all sorts of other things, while Giorgio Chinaglia had been lecturing him on not throwing his life away. Chinaglia had been the George Best of Italy, so talented yet so unconventional a character that he found he found it difficult to adapt to discipline. He didn't want the same thing to happen to Gazza and they had spent most of the evening discussing life's ups and downs.

Just as I was climbing into bed at 12.45 am, the phone rang. It was Sheryl. She was at the Hilton with the kids. She had got to the airport, the kids had been tired and the airport had been busy so she couldn't face going home to nothing. Effectively, as she didn't have a house to go to, it had meant all sorts of problems with the two kids. Her parents were separated, and neither had room for their daughter and two grandchildren. But Sheryl didn't think Paul wanted her back. I spent the next twenty minutes persuading her not to leave on the first flight the next morning, but wait until I got to the hotel to see her. Seeing the state that Paul was in, I was pretty sure that he didn't want her to go. She agreed to wait until the morning before making any decisions.

I then called Paul, who was drunk, and told him to sober up as Sheryl was still in Italy and would be ringing him. He was to stress that Anna and John were here, or Sheryl would think he didn't give two hoots about her and had called his sister over as soon as she was out of the way. A few minutes later Sheryl rang back and said Paul was drunk. This was not incredibly informative news at two in the morning, but I repeated my previous conversation and she agreed to wait until I got to the hotel.

The next morning, the phone rang at eight thirty. It was Paul.

'Where's Sheryl?'

'The Hilton,' I replied. 'How do you feel?'

'Got a headache.'

'I'll bring you some aspirin, then go and talk to Sheryl.'

Gazza was getting desperate. 'Can you sort it out for me?' he pleaded.

He didn't want her to go, but he couldn't cope with any more emotional problems.

I went to the training ground, supplied him with aspirin, then fled to the Hilton, leaving him to get on with the interview.

I talked to Sheryl and finally persuaded her to give it another go. When Paul arrived at the hotel with the television crew in tow, he and Sheryl kissed and made up and it all ended happily ever after – at least that was what I was hoping. I ended up babysitting with my friend Mary and getting to bed at 2 am again.

ALL IN THE FAMILY

I was hoping that the next day would be crisis free. I went to the training ground and had my usual little chat with Paul.

'Is everything alright?' I asked.

He hesitated a moment. 'I think so.'

'You should concentrate on the football.' I said.

'When they allow me to play.'

He was getting ever more frustrated by Lazio's reluctance in letting him loose on the pitch. The England trip to Spain was the only thing that was keeping him going. The thought of seeing his mates again was important to him; he needed to be around people who knew him.

I left him to train and later I called into the Hotel degli Aranci. where the team were staying, to organize Doctor Bartolini's trip to Spain. A worried Maurizio Manzini drew me aside to discuss Paul's behaviour problems. Paul had urinated on the massage table and was doing other even more unrepeatable things in front of the doctors and nurses while being examined. Lazio had never before experienced such infantile behaviour. Even Paul's team-mates had ceased to find it funny, and it was reported that after one particular training session, Paul had come into the dressing room and urinated on some of the players in the shower.

As far as I'm concerned, adults don't do these kind of things unless in they are in a precarious psychological state of mind.

I suggested to Mel and to Lazio that they organize some professional help for Paul, but nothing was ever done, probably for fear of the story getting into the papers. On a more positive note, Sheryl said that she had got him out of making himself sick after meals, just as she had also weaned him off sleeping with the lights on, and comforted him when he had nightmares. Sometimes, he would get overcome by fear and she helped him calm down.

It was back to action stations the following day, as David Platt, Des Walker and Gazza prepared to fly to Spain from Rome to join the England team. I was helping the English FA organize flights and hotels, and taking responsibility for getting them all on the plane on Monday morning.

The Serie A season kicked off on 6 September and Lazio were away to Sampdoria. At this point, it was easy to forget with all the other things going on that Paul Gascoigne was out in Italy to play football. He wasn't part of the team to play against Sampdoria, and Lazio didn't insist on prolonging his misery by forcing him to travel up to Genoa with them. He was undoubtedly frustrated at not being able to play; he thought Lazio were being too cautious. The thigh strain felt better, and he was dying to get back on to a football pitch. He had been made to sit on the sidelines while the team played training matches and he hated it. You felt that he was like an angry bull waiting for the gates to open so he could once again show off his skills in front of an adoring public. For manager Dino Zoff, though, it had been a blessing in disguise. Zoff had the unenviable task of managing four foreign players with only three able to play. That meant one unhappy footballer a week, if all four were fit. He knew there would be pressure on him to play Gascoigne, as soon as he was fit. Lazio were not being overly cautious, they were just protecting their investment, and making sure Gazza didn't come back too quickly.

The two Germans, Thomas Doll and Karlheinz Riedle, were already part of the team, and weren't going to take very kindly to being pushed out. A lot had been made of the com-

petition between the foreigners, but it wasn't really like that.
It was just that Doll, Riedle and Winter all spoke German, so
it was natural for them to stick together. Thomas Doll was too
much like Gascoigne in character to become a good friend.
An extrovert, bubbly East German, he played in a similar role
and it was not always easy for both of them to play in the same
team. However, there was certainly no question of them hat-
ing each other, as some journalists tried to suggest. Gascoigne
managed to mix in with the Italians, especially room-mate
Sclosa and goalkeeper, Fernando Orsi.

The match in Genoa ended in a 3–3 draw. Six goals in one
game wasn't bad, and was a good feast for the people back in
England who had tuned into Channel Four for the live match
from Italy. Gazza reckoned he would make his comeback two
weeks later away against Cagliari, which is where he started
his World Cup adventure two years earlier.

Mel and Len arrived on the last flight from London on the
Sunday night of the Sampdoria match and I went to meet
them from the airport. On the way, I called into the Sheraton
hotel to see if David Platt and Des Walker had arrived. David
was present and correct, Des had yet to show up. I picked up
Mel and Len and drove back to Rome to my flat where they
were both staying. They had come down to attend some publicity meetings I had set up to see if a deal could be struck with
a local milk producing firm. This company had wanted to use
Gazza's face on the cartons of some of their products. Mel and
Len were very keen to see this deal through, as there had been
a lot of money going out of Paul Gascoigne Promotions and
not enough coming in.

The next morning we were up at six. Mel said his morning
prayers, and then we went off to the villa, where Mel and Len
wanted to catch Paul before he left for the airport. We got to
the villa and they just had time to see Paul, before departing
for the airport. Another Mondiapol car was on its way to pick
up David at the Sheraton, and we all arrived and found Des
already in the airport.

Lazio v Genoa and Gazza makes his long-awaited Serie A debut. It proved to be a satisfactory start to his career in Italy, despite a knock on the knee which temporarily silenced the crowd at the Olympic Stadium.

Father and son in their new airconditioned villa in the centre of Rome.

'Gazzamania' hits Rome with a vengeance (*above*), but the message seems lost on our local hero (*left*), his attention firmly focussed on girlfriend Sheryl Kyle.

The Italian's not going too well, so how about a little sign language? Gascoigne in trouble with the referee again.

Lazio's new star can't resist taking the mickey, so down come the shorts of captain Claudio Sclosa after Lazio's triumph over Spurs in the Capital's Cup at White Hart Lane.

Determination from Gazza during the Rome derby (*above*), in which Lazio drew 1-1 with Roma...

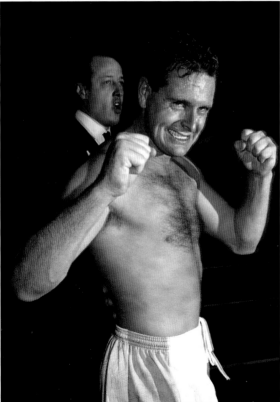

...and in emotional mood after scoring Lazio's late equaliser. Good friend and shadow, Gianni Zeqireya, Captain of Mondiapol, is in close attendance.

In action with team-mates Riedle and Neri (*above*) and a bit on the side for
Gianmarco Calleri (*below*), former chairman of Lazio and the man who wanted
Gazza in his team at any cost.

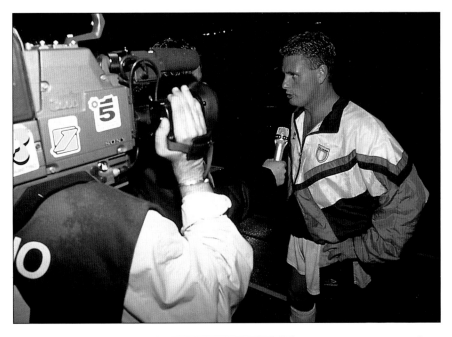

Gazza's interviews with the Italian paparazzi (*above*) are always entertaining affairs, with or without the hot air.

'The Englishman who conquered the hearts of Rome.'

Gazza scores his second and England's fourth goal against Turkey during a 1994 World Cup qualifier (*above*). England won again in Izmir four months later, but there remained doubts about Gazza's fitness, especially from England manager, Graham Taylor (*left*).

Never a dull moment in the England camp with these two around – mud wrestlers Ian Wright and Paul Gascoigne.

San Marino were outclassed by England in February 1993, but Gazza was not at his best (*above left*). After fracturing his cheekbone in the World Cup qualifier against Holland, he was forced to wear a 'Phantom of the Opera' protective mask, but it didn't stop him from playing brilliantly against Ancona (*above right*) as he inspired Lazio to a 5-0 win.

And finally, will it be more pasta…or a return to pie and chips?

It was the first time that all three players had been together in Italy and they were all dying to tell each other about what they thought about Italian football. Des had confessed that the summer training camp had nearly finished him off, it had been nothing like Nottingham Forest. He had never had to train so hard or had such aching muscles; he thought he would never get through the first few days. David, having already had a year in Italy, was the veteran, and you could see the difference. Bodyguard Gianni was walking along the airport concourse with all three of them, when he suddenly turned to me and said: 'This David Platt, he looks like Gazza's manager.' It was true, with his mobile phone, smart Italian designer suit, and confident air, he looked like he would be more at home wheeling and dealing than with a ball at his feet. It was pretty clear that David would have as successful a career off the field when he retired as he had on it. Gazza was clearly happy to be going to join his mates, and even though he wouldn't be part of the team, he would at least be with old friends. The plane was delayed, so David Platt took control of the situation phoning his manager, Tony Stephens and asking him to inform the FA and also David's wife that he would be delayed.

We left David in charge and went back to Rome. With Paul away, I thought I would manage to catch up on the administration and get the office files in order. This lasted less than twenty four hours as on the day of the England match, Paul and Sheryl were back arguing again. This time it was about the fact that he wanted her to change the names of the kids from her married name to her single name, as she was almost divorced. She objected as it meant going back to the school and changing everything. So she put the answerphone on and refused to pick up the phone to Paul, with the result that they both started ringing me.

'What's she said?' was the usual cry from Paul.

'This is not fair on me,' I exclaimed, 'I'll end up taking the blame. You can't interfere in people's relationships without ending up as a troublemaker.'

First thing next morning, when the team had landed and Paul was in Hoddesdon, he rang me as Sheryl was still not speaking to him. Sheryl and Paul had a way of irritating each other – in fact, that was partly the problem. It seemed as if it was two teenagers arguing, and not two adults. I went about organizing his and Carl's tickets. Jimmy, at this point, was in Newcastle and not coming back until he'd sorted out his domestic dispute. Apparently, he had a fight with his girl-friend. Little did I know that Jimmy would not be reappearing on the scene again, until Paul was away on holiday the following year.

I managed to persuade Sheryl to come to the airport with me, and we had dinner in Rome first. She was still unsure as to whether things would last and I had to agree, it seemed as if they were making and breaking up with a speed that wasn't conducive to Paul playing football. Moreover, it seemed as if her insistence on having her own needs catered to was going to always be a difficult part of the relationship. Being involved with a star was obviously not easy, it had its advantages and disadvantages. Usually the wife was an easy-going type, simply because the husband didn't want to come home to a thousand problems, when he had been hassled all day by fans or the press.

'I haven't any close friends out here,' she complained. 'I need someone to talk to.' When I suggested she make friends with the other players' wives, she said Paul wouldn't let her. I couldn't understand who was more at fault. It seemed there just wasn't the respect to make it work.

The next day, John and Carol Gascoigne arrived at the station. I went to pick them up and then we had a cup of tea in a square near my flat, before I took them over to the villa. Sheryl's parents and grandparents were also visiting, so it was quite crowded. There were people sleeping all over the villa: the children were sharing a room, John and Carol were in the room upstairs, Sheryl's grandparents were down in the flat, and her parents in the snooker room. Terry was on another convertible bed somewhere, and so it went on.

The two families didn't hit it off, especially when it came to the mothers. Susan Failes, Sheryl's Mum, was quite an easy-going type, who seemed almost in awe of her daughter. Sheryl's dominant character had come from her father and his side. Her grandmother was very like her, and still very attractive in her seventies. Carol Gascoigne was a woman who had to work hard all her life. With four kids to bring up and a husband who couldn't work after his brain haemorrhage, she had to be strong.

One of the first arguments arose, of all things, over a frying pan. Carol had a fry up and then left a dirty frying pan in the kitchen sink, which Susan then went and washed up. Apparently, Susan had told Sheryl who then told Paul. Paul told his mother not to leave her dirty pans around for other people to clean. Carol was annoyed because she considered it a sneaky thing to do, to go behind her back rather than tell her straight to her face. So she ran into the kitchen, grabbed Susan and warned her in no uncertain terms to leave her frying pan alone, while waving the offending object in her face. I think Susan got the message.

I was witness to the next scene which involved the washing. I arrived at the villa to find the Gascoigne clan lying round the swimming pool and the Failes out. Carol complained that Sheryl's mum had put on the washing machine and mixed the whites and coloureds, so that John's white England tracksuit top was now a kind of murky blue. Carol said that Susan should have minded her own business and not touch things that didn't belong to her. She was obviously quite wound up and it was clear that there was tension between the two families. A short while later, Paul came back with the Failes family and a blazing new row erupted in the kitchen, which ended in Carol rushing out into the garden, shouting and crying. John seemed to think it would sort itself out and stayed by the pool. Carol then went indoors and up to her room. I followed her up there to find her packing. In fact, my life seemed to revolve around suitcases at this time, if it wasn't Sheryl it was Carol. Carol said she wanted to go, and I said that Paul wouldn't like that. Then he came up with Mason, so I took Mason downstairs and let them sort it out, which they eventually did.

I must say that I found Carol's direct approach to life much easier to cope with because she wasn't afraid to say what she felt about a particular situation. You always knew where you stood with Carol, which was important. She had been through a difficult life, and wasn't prepared to see her son's happiness upset by some woman. Carol is not a clingy type of mother, although she did worry about Paul and with reason. She knew when he was happy and when he was not and he clearly wasn't here in Rome. He was struggling to get fit and he had a girlfriend who wasn't sure if she was staying or going. He was doing everything he could to try and make her happy, including having all her family to stay, and entertaining them when it would have been better if he led a quieter life, eating regularly and going to bed early. Paul's ex-girlfriend, Donna, had been adored by everyone. She was an East End girl but with a heart of gold. She never sought the limelight and was always thinking of what would make Paul happy, before thinking of herself. Everyone thought she would be ideal for Paul, but it just wasn't to be.

Paul and Carol soon made it up and some sort of peace returned, although there was an uneasy atmosphere. Lazio, meanwhile, had appointed a new general manager to be responsible for the running of the club. Enrico Bendoni had been the press director from Italia '90, and was a former general manager of Juventus. I had known Enrico since the World Cup as he had been my direct boss, and I was in a good position to judge that he was the right person for the job. Calm and authoritative, he understood how to cope with difficult situations without causing an uproar. One of the first things he wanted to do was meet Gazza and Sheryl. He knew that it would difficult for Gazza to settle into the demanding atmosphere of Rome, and doubly so as the fans had taken him to their hearts and expected a lot from him.

We met in the Hassler hotel one Saturday afternoon, before Sheryl and Paul embarked on one of their shopping expeditions. The meeting was short and cordial. Enrico explained that if Paul had any problems, he was to come to him and he would always try and help him. Paul should feel that the club was behind him, and would help him to obtain the stability he needed to play football. Paul said that the only thing that was important to him was to have Gianni Zeqireya from Mondiapol in close attendance as he was someone Paul could trust and rely on during his settling down period. At this point, the only thing that Paul wanted was to play. He had once again been left out of the side to play Cagliari that day in Lazio's third league match of the season.

When they returned from Cagliari the next day, Lazio had drawn three times in the league, 3–3 with Sampdoria, 2–2 with Fiorentina and 1–1 with Cagliari. Gazza couldn't wait to get back and his debut was planned for the following Wednesday, when he would play in the Lazio versus Tottenham match. In fact, due to contractual obligations, this had to be Gazza's first match for Lazio and it had to be played before 29 September or there would be a massive penalty to pay, close on quarter of a million pounds. There were doubts until the last minute as to whether the match would go ahead or not. There were problems about the television rights, as Sky had bought them and then discovered that both the English and Scottish FA's were protesting using the UEFA rule, banning incoming live matches unless agreed by the home federations, as their reason for protest.

In the midst of all the drama leading up to the match, we did a photo shoot at the top of the Spanish steps for *Esquire* magazine. In a deal set up by Mel Stein, the *Sunday Mirror* magazine and *Esquire* were contracted to hold interviews with Paul Gascoigne in exchange for a four-figure sum each.

But the *Sunday Mirror* magazine was cut out due to the fact that Sheryl wouldn't agree for Paul to be interviewed by Paula Yates! ('She's not getting near Paul,' was Sheryl's response.)

Fortunately, Paul was brilliant during the shoot, which took place in the Hassler hotel. We had a make-up artist along who made him up for the cameras, complete with mascara which was then taken off, as he did look rather effeminate. Being a blond, dark false eyelashes made him look rather odd. The photos, however, came out well. We even had a Ferrari Testarossa on hand outside and did some shots in that.

Mel was disappointed to miss the photo shoot, but he did manage to chat to the journalist while he was waiting for Paul at the training ground and, as a result, got his name in the magazine. He enjoyed being the centre of attention, and always insisted on running all the media contact. Although I had ten years' PR and press experience, the only way I was allowed to get involved was with the Italian press (as he didn't speak enough Italian to communicate fluently) and with the British press on Jewish holidays. It was one of the things we argued most violently about. I just couldn't agree with Mel over trying to get money out of magazines like *Shoot*, and foreign publications such as *France Football* and *Kicker*. An exclusive was different, payment was expected, but this had to be balanced with giving general press conferences so everyone could get some coverage on the client and a balanced image could be built. Tony Stephens, who manages David Platt, is brilliant with the media and can get major life style features in papers like the *Guardian*, which he does for free and which enhances David's image.

The news coverage of Gazza's return was incredible. There were pages and pages of articles about him, about the previous Lazio superstar, Giorgio Chinaglia, details of Gazza's career, his World Cup, hopes for the England team, analysis of his injury, everything. It was the biggest build up to a friendly match imaginable.

Mel, Len and I had a meeting with Lotto on the afternoon of the match in my flat/office to discuss the boot deal, which looked like being agreed. Lotto were very keen to have Paul as one of their players, and were prepared to pay a lot of money for the privilege. They were now in need of a new, younger player to take the place of the veteran Ruud Gullit, who had served them well in publicity terms over the past few years.

'Maltese Kevin' turned up at about 5 pm. He was from the firm in Malta that was setting up Paul's offshore company to protect his commercial earnings. Malta and Italy had a kind of double-tax agreement, so it was a favourable place to have a company. Mel and Len were to set things up and oversee the running of the company. Through all these negotiations, it had been difficult to gauge how much Gazza was taking in, as he was rarely present at these meetings. It was his life, but sometimes it might just as well have been someone else's.

It was time for the match and we all set off for the stadium in the pouring rain. Once there, we met Terry Venables and his wife Yvette, Jonathan Crystal, Gino Santin and Lawrie McMenemy, who had come over to see Paul in his first match playing for Lazio against Tottenham in the Capitals' Cup. Lawrie was rooting for Paul, coming from the same part of the country he understood the problems and the jealousies he had to put up with. It was also a poignant moment for Terry to see his former protégé play for another club.

Paul came on to the pitch and was immediately in his element. It was just like being back in England, the rain was falling in torrents and he was playing against an English team, even if it was his old side, Tottenham Hotspur. It only took eleven minutes for Gazza to make his mark on the game. A cross from the right by Doll found Gazza with space just inside the Tottenham penalty, from where he jubilantly planted the ball in the back of the net past goalkeeper, Ian Walker. The 25,000 crowd went mad. It was like a fairy tale, the injured warrior had returned and scored in the magnificent Olympic stadium, scene of the final of the 1990 World Cup.

Lazio won the match 3–0, with further goals from Stroppa and Neri, and Gazza came off after sixty-eight minutes. He was in such a good frame of mind that he decided to amuse himself by throwing bottles of water at the photographers who tried to get near him on the bench, soaking them all.

There had been a moment of tension during the match as Lazio stretched their lead and Mel had loudly criticized Tottenham for being a waste of his time. Terry Venables immediately voiced his objection to this comment, which he felt had been grossly unfair, especially in view of the fact that several key members of his side were injured. Jonathan Crystal agreed with Terry. It was an incident that could have been avoided.

What this friendly match had proved was that Gazza still had the class and the ability to play as before. The twists and turns and close control of the ball were still there, now he had to get match fit. Only by playing competitive matches could he hope to do that. This became a problem for Zoff as it meant that he had to use Gazza even when he wasn't completely ready, so that the player could regain full fitness. This involved sacrificing one of the other foreign players, since only three could be named in the team.

Paul threw a party afterwards to celebrate. He was very relaxed, but not overwhelmed. He never had any doubts that he would be back. At 1.15 in the morning we left the superstar quietly brushing out the kitchen. He was sober and happy.

It was soon Sheryl's birthday and Paul asked me to book a table at the Hassler and order a cake, which I did. However, things were not going well again. Although he had bought her a huge bunch of flowers, she was not happy, and when left alone in the villa while the others had all gone to the training ground, she started to get fed up. The result was that they went to the rooftop restaurant at the Hassler, argued, had a drink and then left. The evening had not been a success.

There was tension on the pitch as well. Dino Zoff wouldn't confirm if Paul was going to play or not on Sunday, and during a practice match, a group of English journalists saw him throw his training bib down and stalk off. I arrived after the incident and Dino Zoff assured me it had been nothing, Paul had just been disappointed as his side had lost. But it was enough to put Gazza's nerves on edge and he threatened the journalists that he wouldn't talk to them again if they wrote rubbish.

The next day, the headlines in the English press were about the training ground incident. An over-enthusiastic photographer had told his news desk, so the press had been forced to write about it.

Gazza repeated once more that he was ready to play again, and chairman Sergio Cragnotti had said he wanted to see Gazza playing against Genoa. This left Dino Zoff in a difficult position. If he didn't play Gazza and Lazio lost, the coach would be buried. If he played him and they lost, he would be criticized for giving in to pressure from the fans and his chairman. He would leave his decision to the last possible minute.

The following day Gazza wasn't speaking to the press, either English of Italian, but he seemed more relaxed. It appeared that his league debut was only a day away. Zoff had indicated that Gazza would play and so finally he would get a chance to establish himself in the Italian league. The only sad part was that John and Carol Gascoigne had gone home and wouldn't see their son's Serie A debut. It appeared that Paul, even though he wasn't aware of it at the time, was being forced to take a stand between his family and Sheryl's, and for the time being his family were losing out.

YES, PRIME MINISTER

On the Saturday, the team left for the Hotel degli Aranci as usual. Unlike their English counterparts, an Italian team would always spend the previous day and night before a match together either in a hotel, or at their training ground if they had the facilities. Paul Gascoigne didn't like these enforced stays in hotels. He found them boring as he couldn't understand the language.

Before he went off with the team, I helped Paul write a letter to the Prime Minister to tell him about the tree planting ceremony that Paul was involved in for the unification of Europe, and also to invite the PM to the return match of the Capitals' Cup, which was to be played at White Hart Lane on 20 October.

Dear John,

['A bit informal,' I commented, but Gazza said, 'No, he's a good lad.' The Prime Minister had obviously succeeded in obtaining Gazza's approval!]

I am delighted to be involved [Jane dictating] with Beacon Europe and will be planting 12 trees at the Lazio training ground for the unification of Europe.

Lazio are playing Tottenham in London on 20 October. I would really like you to come and watch me play, because [and here I paused, and Gazza took over] it will be a change from watching Mellor perform in a Chelsea strip!

Best wishes and Good Luck.

Paul Gascoigne

P. S. See you in October.

I thought twice about sending it, then thought why not, it was natural and it was typical Gazza – no malice, just a little joke which the PM might find amusing among the drudge of general business. I sent a covering letter and off it went. Three weeks later, we got a reply from John Major, which said he was sorry he couldn't attend the match due to other commitments, but he wished Paul luck. At the end of the letter was a handwritten note saying, 'Welcome back to the England team'. He was human after all.

The team bus left and I went about organizing the chores. At five o'clock I rang Paul.

'How are you?'

'Bored,' came Gazza's sullen reply. 'Can you ring Carl and get him to bring some videos over?'

'OK, what film are you going to see?' I knew that Italian teams usually went to the cinema on Saturday afternoons.

'That's a waste of time as well. I won't be able to understand a word.'

'What is it?' I persisted.

'Basic Instinct.'

I laughed. 'You don't have to know much Italian to understand that!'

On the Sunday of the Lazio–Genoa match, there were still doubts as to whether Gazza would play. I spoke to him at 9.20 am and he was spitting mad.

'The villa gates are f---ing stuck. I went to the training ground to meet Sheryl to get some videos to watch and she wasn't there – she couldn't get out of the house.'

I said I would contact the owner of the house to have it put right. For such a high rent, you wouldn't expect such things to be going wrong.

I rang Paul again from the stadium at 1 pm and he seemed in good form. We arranged that he would only speak to the television after the match and he asked if I could be around for that. It seemed as if he was definitely playing. The question of whether Gazza would make his Serie A debut was occupying pages and pages in both the English and Italian press. It was also giving Graham Taylor a few headaches, as he had no idea whether Paul would be fit to play in the World Cup qualifier against Norway in October.

As Lazio came out onto the pitch, any further doubts were laid to rest when the figure of a well-known Geordie was spotted in the line up. Aron Winter had been the foreigner to drop out of the team for Gazza's debut. This should have been the day of Gazza's triumphant return to league football. However, it didn't quite turn out like that. He was still a long way short of being match fit, and after a good first twenty minutes when we saw some of the old Gazza – a couple of perfect crosses for his team-mates, a shimmy past his marker, a solo dribble through the Genoa defence – he faded into the background.

Approaching half-time, there was a heartstopping moment when Genoa defender Bortolazzi crashed into Gazza, sending the English player sprawling to the ground. Gazza got up in a flash, then went down again. For one dreadful moment, it felt like we were reliving the Wembley injury. A fearful hush came over the Olympic stadium

As soon as referee Trentalange realized who was down, he sprinted over to Gazza. Then a remarkable thing happened. The Genoa players all crowded round to see if Gazza was all right, and put their arms round him as he stood up and limped about to test the leg. Bortolazzi was one of the first to ask him if he was okay and offer his apologies. It was a moment that demonstrated the other side of the hard face of Italian football, the human side, in which fellow professionals had shown compassion. The fear of crippling injury was a fear shared by all footballers, and the Genoa players wanted Gazza to know that they understood and admired his courageous fightback to fitness. It is one of the few times that the competitiveness of a game had been overtaken by a communal human spirit of affection and concern.

Gazza had, in fact, only picked up a 'dead leg', but even he had been frightened by the experience as he had lost all feeling below the knee. Afterwards, he said to me that as soon as he went down he noticed the silence and sensed the fear of the fans, so he had tried to get up as quickly as possible to let them know he was all right.

Erring on the cautious side, Zoff substituted Gascoigne with Sclosa at half-time and the match finished in a 1–1 draw, the fourth draw in a row for Lazio. Lazio captain Gregucci had scored after thirteen minutes with Padovano equalizing for Genoa in the second half.

In Rome, Zoff was under pressure. The fans expected the team to win at home, not just draw. The week started off under a cloud of tension. The fans turned up at the training ground to make their discontent known and the press criticized the team's overall performance, with special blame reserved for the Lazio defence.

There was morning and afternoon training on the Wednesday. Gazza seemed agitated and it felt like there was a storm brewing. Sure enough, I arrived at the training ground in the afternoon just as Paul was storming out of the ground to his car, with Mason beside him.

I followed him home to find out what had happened. Arriving at the villa, I discovered Paul in his bath robe, with Sheryl nowhere in sight. He didn't know where she was, so I sat Mason on my knee and fed him cake and let Paul talk about his problems. He admitted to feeling tense and that he was fed up with certain aspects of the training. There was a lack of commitment from some of the players and it irritated him. 'They just don't take it seriously,' he muttered disconsolately. (As an 11-year-old at Breckenbeds Junior High, Paul had been similarly frustrated by the lack of effort of some of his mates. A former teacher recalls Paul 'ran himself into the ground for the team and expected the others to do the same'.) Paul also hated the feeling of being seventeen all over again and having to fight for a place in the team. He knew he was the best player and it frustrated him to have to sit and wait and not know until the last minute whether he would play. He wanted Zoff to tell him well before the match, so he could prepare himself mentally for the situation.

The dog was wandering in and out looking hopeful. The problem with her presence seemed to have disappeared and Paul had accepted her and was feeding her. I thought about what to do. It seemed wise to involve Lazio, as this was essentially a club problem and not related to his life off the pitch. So I rang Enrico Bendoni and Maurizio Manzini, and it was decided that Maurizio and I would return that evening to talk to Paul.

Sheryl turned up with Bianca and, while Paul was having a shower, told me she had been sitting outside the training ground to see if Paul spoke to any of the female fans that hung about outside. I told her I thought it was highly unlikely, as the way he had belted out of the training ground, he wouldn't have seen Claudia Schiffer if she had been standing naked, waving to him. It seemed like Sheryl needed constant reassurance, but Paul himself was going through hell at Lazio, and was under tremendous pressure to perform.

I drove back to the training ground, picked up Maurizio and we returned to the villa to discuss Paul's problems with the training and match preparation, with Sheryl present as well. This went on until 9.45 pm, by which time Paul was feeling a lot better. Maurizio had given him assurances that he was a very important player for Lazio, and everyone was very happy with his progress. The next day they would sort it all out with Zoff.

Lazio said they would prefer it if Paul remained in Italy to continue his progress towards peak fitness rather than go to England to play in the forthcoming World Cup qualifier, but they couldn't, of course, refuse the English FA request. I decided not to cause chaos by pushing the decision, as Graham Taylor was due to name his squad the next day, and I knew Paul was dying to get away for a few days and be with his old mates.

The next morning, I did ring Paul to say that Lazio would like it if he could stay in Rome, instead of going back to England. His reply was short and to the point. He said he wanted to go and they could 'get stuffed'. I conveyed this to Lazio in diluted form and it was decided that it was best to let him go off to join England, and say nothing.

At 10 am, Sheryl phoned in tears to say that she'd had enough and was off home again. She said she was going back to England when Paul went next week to sort out a flat. The game-playing of jealousy and suspicion was getting them both down, and I had to agree that it was better if they split up. Paul needed serenity and love; he didn't need to be questioned about who he had spoken to at the training ground and if he was looking at other girls. It was obvious he was worried out of his mind about the playing side, and needed reassurance. Sheryl, on her part, needed to be reassured that she was number one. It had irritated her that he would exclude her from football chat and turn to his mates to talk for hours on the telephone, but that was the way of life in Italian football. She had to learn to trust him or go home, It was really as simple as that.

Dino Zoff wouldn't say whether Paul would be in the team for Sunday's match against Parma. I gave Paul a little card telling him to think of his future and not let anything get him down. It seemed to cheer him up, and he promised to put it up in the dressing room.

I had lunch with Telemontecarlo to discuss a proposal for Paul to do a series of interviews and participate in their programmes for a fee. It was a feasible proposition but the only problem was that it was proving difficult to get him to do one programme a week. He was very good at television presenting, but didn't like to do anything that interfered too much with his football. My brief was to obtain a couple of big publicity contracts for as little participation on Paul's part as possible (so we could do a couple of television spots, but no being dragged round openings and exhibitions). It wasn't as easy as it seemed, as there had to be a solid base of good media coverage before a company outside the immediate football world would invest money in using a personality to promote its products. In fact, several large companies refused to use individuals on the basis that they could be unreliable in image as well as attendance. In Paul's case, it was often difficult to persuade companies that he was a serious proposition because of his reputation as a bit of a hellraiser.

We finally did the Channel Four television recording, which went well, and during which I was able to present Paul with the watch that Telemontecarlo had asked me to give to him. His team-mates immediately took it into the dressing room and covered it with shaving foam. We had to get through everything fairly quickly as Paul had promised Sheryl that he wouldn't be late home so they could go food shopping.

That evening I planned to go out to dinner with some friends from Lazio, Giorgio Catalano and his wife, Antonella, both of whom I had worked with at Italia '90, and attended their wedding when they had married after the World Cup, and Lazio marketing manager, Tommaso Cellini. I was having a shower, when there was a panic call from Paul. Sheryl hadn't turned up and he had to get to the Villa Miani, where Lazio Chairman, Sergio Cragnotti, was hosting a dinner for the players. Paul had already missed the team coach from the training ground and didn't want to be seen as being different from the lads. He had no idea of the location of Villa Miani and was in a real state, having been sick with nerves and worry. I told him to get to the Hilton as it was literally two minutes away from the hotel and I would get him to the dinner, and then take the kids back home. As my car was parked in a garage 10 minutes walk from my house, I jumped into a taxi and dashed off to the Hilton. Luckily, the taxi driver was a Lazio fan. He thought he had seen Thomas Doll in Piazza Spagna the previous day, and was thrilled at the prospect of meeting Paul. We set off and got to the Hilton in record breaking time, taking shortcuts through car parks. I phoned the villa on the driver's mobile phone and Sheryl answered. She had been delayed at the shops and got back to find Paul in a panic. He was on his way to the Hilton, and sure enough a few minutes later her white Y10 came hurtling round the corner, with Gazza at the wheel.

We did manage to get him to the dinner on time that night. I was shattered by the whole situation in Rome, the pace seemed to be relentless and the only light at the end of the tunnel was that Paul was off to England the following week and I would finally get some time to start chasing commercial deals. I wasn't complaining, but Mel and Len had also made it clear they wanted to start negotiating deals.

I spoke to Graham Taylor and told him I would try and get a decision out of Dino Zoff the next day as to whether Paul was playing or not, and then ring Graham, so he knew whether to come out or not. The next day, Karlheinz Riedle was still injured, so Paul definitely would be playing. Once more, the stage was set for Gazza. The fans were hungry for a win, and he was hungry to play.

From the Hotel degli Aranci. Paul rang me to say he was concerned as no-one was answering his phone and as it was absolutely deluging down, he presumed that it wasn't working. Sheryl had her friends, John and Wendy Clarke, staying with her, and he was probably worrying about what she was up to. Knowing that he was under intense pressure and didn't need other things on his plate, I dashed off to the villa, where I found Sheryl all dressed up and ready to go out, and the phone not working. She said she would ring Paul when she got to the restaurant. I then drove to the team hotel and delivered some English papers to him and reported that all was well. (I didn't say that Sheryl was all done up and ready to take on the world.) I was in the reception area when Dino Zoff, Enrico Bendoni, Giorgio and Claudio Bartolini came through. Zoff looked surprised to see me and I had to explain that there been an emergency with telephones and Paul had been worried about Sheryl. He sighed, and muttered that he should be thinking about his football, and then looked resigned. It had been apparent from the start that Paul was no ordinary person and had his own needs and worries. Lazio had got so used to seeing me around the place that I'd become a kind of honorary team member. I think Zoff half expected to see me lying curled up outside Gazza's bedroom door waiting for the next set of instructions.

I sauntered home and the next day met Graham Taylor at the Hilton to bring him up to date on progress so far.

'He's frustrated at not playing, and he's having difficulties with Sheryl,' I said.

'That's why I'm here,' Graham replied, 'I want him to know he's still very important to England.

Graham Taylor was giving Gazza all the support he possibly could, he was determined to stick by him and show he cared. He felt protective towards his star talent.

We went on to the Hotel degli Aranci and briefly saw the team, before they left for the Olympic stadium. Gazza had been particularly pleased to see Graham Taylor. On the way to the stadium Graham predicted that it would be a 0–0 draw. We took our places in the VIP box and witnessed one of Lazio's best matches to date.

In midfield and attack Lazio were looking strong, but when it came to defending they still looked a little unsure. Yet this was the day of the striker. Lazio's Italian international, Beppe Signori, scored a hat-trick, taking his goal tally to seven in only five matches. Gascoigne himself had a magic hour. He'd found his ideal position, in the space behind the two strikers

Signori and Doll, and with Winter at his shoulder like a guiding angel. Gazza surprisingly (as they had similar playing styles) struck it off with Thomas Doll, as he launched the German on a series of raids inside the Parma penalty area. After only 13 minutes Lazio were awarded a penalty for a foul on Gascoigne, which Signori took and put away neatly into the net. Lazio were now on the boil and Diego Fuser, who put on a great show throughout, scored Lazio's second 12 minutes later. Parma then pulled back a goal through Osio only for Signori to score his second to make it 3–1. It was Fuser again who increased the lead for Lazio in the 37th minute before Osio replied right on half-time to make it 4–2 to Lazio. And there were another 45 minutes to go!

Twenty-two minutes into the second half Zoff substituted a tiring Gazza, who came off the field to a standing ovation. It had been his finest hour so far in Italian football. We had seen some of the old Gazza: the leader shouting to his men to get forward, the precise passes, the sharp twists and turns, and the close control and dribbling skills. The Olympic stadium had been thrilled. At the end of the match, which Lazio won 5–2, Gazza was taken by a team-mate to stand in front of the terraces to receive the accolade of the fans. Finally, this seemed like a team going places.

Graham Taylor was delighted and promised Gazza a place in the England team for their next match 'I'm very proud. To return to playing for my country makes me very happy,' Gascoigne said in reply. We were gathered in a little room opposite the players' lounge. It was Graham Taylor's first opportunity to meet Sheryl, and he also noticed how influential she was on Gazza, who listened to what she said and followed her every move. 'He looks to her constantly for reassurance and guidance,' was Graham's comment as we walked back to the car. The troubles of the previous week seemed temporarily forgotten and we all hoped Paul and Sheryl would manage to patch things up.

The next day, I called in to Lazio to pick up the document

that Paul had to sign to receive his signing-on fee. Being an extremely straight club, Lazio had paid tax on this amount and registered the document with the Italian Football Federation. It was a lot of money and I hoped it wouldn't all go down the drain. Paul was very generous and Sheryl liked beautiful things, and the two weren't conducive to a healthy bank balance. He was also very benevolent to all his family and friends, so I hoped that Mel and Len were investing wisely and he'd have plenty left for when he retired. Once superstardom faded, then he'd discover who his true friends were.

Jimmy had not returned from Newcastle and Mel had informed him that his presence wasn't required. I had felt very sorry for Jimmy, he was a good and loyal friend, a bit of a rascal, but not bad, and totally devoted to Paul. He would have done anything for Paul as he had proved, and he was always there for him whenever Paul needed him. I felt Paul hadn't had the courage to tell Jimmy to his face that he wasn't coming back had stuck in my throat. It seemed that Jimmy's presence just wasn't required. If it had been left like that, then Jimmy would probably have returned and some compromise would have been worked out.

For his part, Jimmy was devastated and couldn't understand what he had done wrong. He did eventually come out to Rome the following year, but Gazza was on holiday at the time so they never got together. One day Paul would count the cost of leaving his friends behind.

The following week was also hectic. Lazio had a Cup game against Cesena, and Paul had to go away with the team on the day of Mason's birthday. He asked me to go to the bank for him and then meet him at the training ground before the team left at 3 pm.

My trips to the bank on Paul's behalf were becoming a regular habit. One time, when his parents were staying he'd needed some extra money.

'Can you draw some money out of the bank for me?' he asked.

'Okay, how much?'

'Sixteen grand.'

So here was I travelling around Rome in my car with £16,000 stuffed under the driver's seat, and trying to look natural. I'm sure, to Gazza, it was like pocket money.

Lazio drew away to Cesena 1–1, with yet another goal from the prolific Signori, and the day after the match Gazza left to join the England team. Sheryl had decided to go back to England on the Sunday and decide what to do. The relationship had reached breaking point.

'I feel excluded from his life,' she complained. 'He goes off to phone his family and friends without telling me anything.'

Lazio had a friendly match near Perugia on the Thursday afternoon, and they wanted Paul to go along and do a PR job. As he was on international duty on the Wednesday night, he was dead against it. 'Tell Lazio they can stick the match up their arse,' Gazza said eloquently. Having paid a lot of money for him, Lazio were determined to make the most of their investment, so it was made clear that he had no choice.

Meanwhile, I was at the villa with Marica, who was babysitting the children. After my conversation with Paul, Sheryl rang back to say that Paul had been mad at me because I'd said it was 'Paul' and not 'Daddy' to Mason, when I'd called him to the phone! This was ridiculous as I'd been answering someone else's question as to who was on the phone and Mason was in the garden. I also felt it was a bloody cheek as I was doing them a favour by being there in the first place. I said all this to Sheryl, which could have been the thing that sparked off her supposed dislike of me. I spoke to Paul again and he was fine, so I don't know who was getting at who. Perhaps this was one of the problems. Paul was the type who would moan half-heartedly about people and then forget it and go on to other things, Sheryl tended to blow everything out of proportion, winding him up until he did something about it, whereas if he'd been left alone, he would have moaned and muttered and then let things carry on as normal. At the time I didn't understand why Sheryl had been so cross about the Paul and Daddy bit, but as I got to know them better, it became apparent that if Paul was Lazio's guarantee for a better future, Mason was her's even if it hadn't been planned that way. Paul loved Mason as his own son, and would never leave while Mason continued to think of him as his dad.

The next day, I went to see Giancarlo Guerra, director of Finance for Lazio Football Club, and we discussed various companies that could be interested in sponsoring Paul. Maurizio Manzini had already left for England to join the team and monitor Paul's progress. Paul was still against returning immediately after the match.

Graham Taylor had by this time built up a very good relationship with Lazio, and both sides were extremely open and co-operative. This was an extremely important part of Paul's rehabilitation into the England team, and Lazio were appreciative of the level of access that they had while Paul was with his national team. They felt comfortable and the England team benefited from this close rapport.

I was out that evening and when I got back Marica said Paul had rung to speak to Mason, but he was already in bed, and Marica wasn't going to get him up again. Sheryl had then rung to say that Paul had wanted to speak to Mason. In that case why hadn't they phoned when they knew the children were still up?

On the day of the England game both children were playing up. Bianca wanted to know when her mother was coming back, so I told her she'd be back the next day. When we got in from school, Bianca wanted to speak to her mother, so we rang Wendy Clarke's house, but they'd already left for Wembley. That night it took an hour and a half to get Bianca to go to sleep as she was hysterical. Eventually, she went to sleep when Marica suggested that I tell her I was tired and wanted to go to sleep. Bianca seemed to understand what I was saying to her and turned over and dozed off.

That evening we watched Paul's return to the England team on Sky television. He played very well, and was back to his usual decisive style of play. It made all the difference to the team to have Gazza back in midfield prompting the others. His ability to break free with the ball and run at the Norwegian defence while his colleagues in midfield covered him was an important contribution to the game. England scored first through Platt and seemed in control, but the Norwegians came back in the second half and snatched a late equalizer through Rekdal to make the final score 1–1. Overall, it was a disappointing result for England, yet Gazza's performance had been a positive aspect of the game, despite the fact that he was booked. Taylor had shown that he was willing to build the team around Gazza, and the returning hero had loved it. It seemed as if the progress to full recovery was going better than planned.

The next day, I took the children to school for the last time as Sheryl was going to pick them up that afternoon. As we were driving along we saw a man filling up a bucket by a fountain. Bianca wanted to know what he was doing, and I said he was probably going to wash his car. This sparked off a sudden discussion about her real father. Bianca told me Colin was her real father and was in England, and that Paul Gascoigne wasn't her real father. Mason started jumping up and down at this point shouting 'Paul, Paul', and I thought my days were probably numbered. I could imagine Paul coming home and Mason taking one look at him and asking 'Who are you?' Bearing in mind the violent reaction when I'd referred to Paul by his name and not 'Daddy', it would have been better if I'd just slipped off and quietly committed hari kari along the via Veneto.

Sheryl arrived back and went to pick the children up. She was concerned about how they'd been, and happy that her relationship with Paul seemed to be on a new, more secure footing.

'He's been very affectionate, he's said some incredible things, he promised me I was the most important thing in his life.'

He also had put a large amount of money into her bank account, as insurance against them splitting up and so she would have enough money for renting somewhere in England. She had said she would give it a month to see how it would go. She also said that she didn't want to live in the villa any more, and Paul had said they could change houses. I doubted very much if Mel or Len would allow Paul to throw away the money that had been paid in advance for the rent, but we would see. At least it all seemed to be lovey dovey again.

Maurizio had managed to drag Paul back to Italy on the first flight, so he had gone off to Perugia and done his PR bit for the club. This was important in maintaining a good relationship with the fans, as there were several big clubs in that area. They'd driven for nearly three hours through the green countryside of Italy and Paul had sat obediently on the bench and watched the match.

Graham Taylor rang me to discuss a few things that had occurred during the England team get together. Paul's phone bill had run into thousands of pounds and by now everyone including Graham was getting worried about his relationship with Sheryl.

'I don't know what's up,' Graham said. 'One night he was on the phone to her and the discussion got louder and louder until he was in tears, and the entire hotel had heard what was going on.

'Another time we were off training and he was on the phone to Sheryl, when he called me over...' Graham's voice rose in a disbelieving tone, '...and put me on to her so I could tell her we really were going training. It's unbelievable!'

Graham Taylor was clearly very concerned about the whole situation. He was trying desperately to be supportive of Gazza, building the team round him, cajoling him and generally spending more time with him than any other player. Yet Gazza still didn't seem to be able to hold things together. It was slowly beginning to all get too much for the England manager. After all, he had a whole team to worry about.

Sunday was the big match, AC Milan against Lazio, and Paul was in the team. Lazio left on Saturday and from Milan, they were due to fly to London to compete in the other half of the Capitals' Cup with a match on Tuesday 20 October at White Hart Lane. It had been my intention to fly to London with the team and do a few marketing things for Paul and Lazio, like organize the Lazio merchandising at the Tottenham shop, and if required, arrange a press conference for the chairman Sergio Cragnotti, who had a merchant bank in London.

But Mel Stein faxed me saying that Paul would be embarrassed if I travelled with the team. If Lazio were willing to pay the expenses, Mel suggested, then maybe they could send me from Rome. Not surprisingly, Lazio didn't show much interest in taking me to London, so I didn't go. However, Sheryl Kyle did go, at Gazza's expense.

Milan beat Lazio 5–3, Signori getting on the scoresheet twice and Winter scoring the other Lazio goal. Milan's Dutch striker, Marco Van Basten, scored two of his side's goals to keep him in touch with Signori at the head of the league's top goalscorers chart. Karlheinz Riedle had been less than happy at being left out of the Lazio team, and Cragnotti was not pleased with the way Lazio played, especially with the defence. As for Gascoigne, he didn't excel as he had done two weeks earlier and Milan had things well under control for most of the match. The result left Lazio still behind Milan, Inter and Juventus in the battle for the league title.

As a consolation prize, I got to stay at the villa and do the school run. On the Monday I passed by Lazio and was in for a shock. The villa that Paul had rented was going into the hands of the court as the owner had creditors who were trying to get their money back and the villa had been put in the hands of a judge who would decide its future. The owner had permission to use it for his own use, but conveniently forgot this, and forgot that he could have gone to the judge and said he had someone willing to pay rent, and the judge could have agreed and the money could have gone towards paying his debts. The lawyers acting on behalf of the creditors had gone to the villa and discovered that someone was living in it, so they had found out who it was and called Lazio. As was usually the case in a crisis, it was a Jewish holiday so I couldn't call Mel. I hadn't the nerve to tell Paul, so I decided to ring Gianni Zeqireya, who sent a security guard round to protect the house and us as I was worried about the owner or the creditors trying to get access and frightening the children. Fortunately, in Italy the legal process took a long time to complete, and after I'd spoken to our lawyer in Rome, Carla Vissat, it seemed as if Paul would be able to see the year out before being expelled. It was yet another instance of things going wrong when Gazza was involved.

Paul had a photo shoot in London for a project called 'Shoot from the hip', which involved photo montage and which should have been very successful in Italy, where they go mad about having signed photos. The idea was to take a photo of Paul which would then be processed so when a fan came to have his or her photo taken, the photo would come out as though he or she was sitting with Paul. It was a great idea which unfortunately was to die a death due to the bureaucratic nightmare of putting it all together. Yet another project to fall by the wayside, it was the end of October and we still hadn't managed to attract any big sponsors.

I'd just got in when Paul rang me. I asked if everything was all right and he said yes, he was showing the players around London. He assured me that he would do the shoot. I asked him where he was and he said at the barbers. It wasn't until I'd put the phone down and glanced at my watch that I realized that he was already late for the shoot. He'd obviously had a sudden crisis of conscience about letting me down as I'd arranged the shoot and called, but he hadn't told me why he'd called. I rang the Hyde Park hotel and let the people who were waiting for him know, and eventually it went ahead with him.

On the Tuesday night, Lazio won the Capitals' Cup after their match against Tottenham at White Hart Lane. Gazza had been acting the clown all evening, and at the end of the game when team-mate Claudio Sclosa was lifting up the Cup in celebration, a certain Geordie prankster in the Lazio strip crept up behind Sclosa's back, grabbed hold of the player's shorts and proceeded to pull them down to his ankles. The crowd went wild. Gazza was back.

Paul and Sheryl returned late the next afternoon, with friend Terry Bailey, Linda Lusardi's husband. Paul had stayed behind when the team had flown back first thing in the morning, as sister Anna had lost the baby she was expecting. He was bitterly upset and wanted to see her and make sure she was alright.

I left for London for a few days and when I returned things were still calm between Paul and Sheryl. Whilst in London, I'd seen Gary and Michelle Lineker and baby George, and suggested they come down to Rome for the derby match at the end of November, especially as it was Gary's birthday, and would be the last one before he left for Japan the following March to play in the J-league. It would also be a chance for Gary to see Gazza play and find out how he was settling in. They decided it would be fun and we agreed to organize it all.

As soon as I got back to Rome, it was decided to go ahead and plant the famous 12 trees for the unification of Europe on the following Monday at the new training ground which was being built at Formello. Gazza asked Zoff for the following Tuesday off so he could go to Eurodisney with Sheryl and the children. Zoff agreed.

The next league match for Lazio was away to Udinese. Meanwhile, *Il Corriere dello Sport* had run an article asking the late names of football what they thought of Gazza. The result was universally in favour. Helenio Herrera said he was

'Great, amongst the top five players in the world.' Cesare Maldini, manager of the Italian Under-21 team agreed 'He's English only from the point of view of his passport. Italy has already filled him with enthusiasm.' The match itself ended in a dull 0–0 draw, with Gazza having an average game. Lazio were lying in mid-table and struggling to make qualification for Europe.

On the Monday we awoke to pouring rain and a thunderstorm – a great day to plant trees! Paul turned up with Gianni Zeqireya having left a message that he'd see me at Formello. Graham Roberts, Consul General of the British Embassy in Rome, came along as guest of honour. It was an exercise not only to promote the unification of Europe, but also to please the local council, who were important as the new training ground was being built in their area. Paul, Sheryl, Bianca and Mason all came to Formello as they were off to the airport as soon as the ceremony was over. Paul looking very smart in a pair of green cords and a natty yellow jumper, did his bit and planted one tree as a symbol of the unification of Europe. Planting all twelve was a little ambitious as it really was bucketing down.

By the Thursday, whether due to the soaking he got planting the tree, or whether he had just picked up a passing bug, Paul was flat out in bed with a high temperature and a bad dose of the 'flu. The team doctor was sent round and Paul was told to stay in bed. Lazio were due to play in Spain against Maradona's team, Seville, the following Tuesday or Thursday, and so it was vital that Gazza was fit.

Sheryl was angry because she said Lazio were using Paul in the Maradona match, as the press were building it up as Maradona against Gascoigne, not Lazio against Seville. Mel Stein said he would do what he could to get more money out of the club. Bearing in mind that Gazza was earning a reputed £4 or £5 million over five years, and was on a large bonus to win the Italian Cup, one presumed he was being paid to not only play for Lazio, but also act as an ambassador. Her hatred of football, I felt, was becoming a problem.

He still wasn't much better the next day and I called round to see him. Sheryl was out and he was complaining that he had back ache. As he'd had a very high temperature I thought it could be his kidneys.

'Have you been drinking enough?' I asked him.

He looked surprised. 'I haven't had anything for over 24 hours.' A light suddenly switched on in his head. 'I'll have a beer.'

'I think you'd better have mineral water,' I smiled.

Lawrie McMenemy rang to see if there was any chance of him playing on the Sunday, as he wanted to come out and see him. Lawrie was worried, especially as the Turkey match was looming.

Fortunately, the next day the dying man sprang out his bed and even managed to attend training. We had a meeting with Enrico Bendoni, and Paul asked if all his team-mates could be paid a bonus from the Maradona match. He had never been greedy where his team-mates were concerned, and if he was going to get money, then so would they. There was a players' committee consisting of five team members, including the captain Gregucci. Gascoigne wasn't part of the set-up as he didn't speak Italian and had to get used to how the whole team structure worked in Italy. He didn't realize that things were different in Italian football. On the eve of the Sunday match, when the players refused to push the management about payments as they wanted to concentrate on the game, Gazza ran up the hotel stairs shouting at Signori and Cravero, 'You haven't got any balls!' The two Italians looked silently at each other.

Paul said he was thinking of going to Eurodisney after the match, and then flying down to Seville for the Maradona match. Dino Zoff had said no, but apparently Paul had spoken to Mel and there was still a lot of money outstanding on his contract, so he was thinking of going anyway. I said nothing to Lazio about Paul's proposed Eurodisney adventure.

The next day, he went to the stadium with the team, but an hour before the match the team doctor discovered he had a temperature and he was sent home. At this point I was not at all concerned about Paul going to Eurodisney as he hadn't been well enough to play, so I couldn't imagine that he'd still go, even though I knew Sheryl wanted to go and take the children. When I got home that evening, my answerphone resembled a telephone switchboard. I had messages from both Enrico Bendoni and Maurizio Manzini. Apparently, team doctor Claudio Bartolini and Maurizio had called round to the villa to check up on Paul, and found him in a taxi on his way to the airport with Sheryl and her offspring. They had followed them to the airport and pleaded with Paul not to go, but both Sheryl and Paul refused to tell them which hotel they were going to. Maurizio had then called Enrico, who called me. I called Mel, who said, yes, he knew where he was and as he was going to stay in Paris until everything was sorted out as far as the outstanding payments were concerned.

Lazio were furious, but helpless. At first they said they would send a couple of people to Paris to haul him back, and I had to try and keep a straight face. I could imagine the whole thing dissolving into a Pink Panther film, with Lazio managers and French security guards trying to catch Gazza, as he came hurtling down the slides or round the big wheel. 'There he goes, catch him!' they would cry as they dodged to avoid Mickey Mouse and Donald Duck.

However, on the other hand I could also understand the gravity of the situation. He had disobeyed his club. If this was Juventus or AC Milan, he would now be given a huge fine and threatened with a one-way ticket home. The question was, what would Lazio do? They were angry but they also needed him to play against Maradona and Seville. As I had been instructed to be at the offices early the next morning, it wasn't long before I discovered the answer.

FANTASYLAND

The next morning I was summoned to see Lazio director general and my old boss, Enrico Bendoni. Enrico is a very balanced person and a clever manager. Italians in power, especially from Rome and the south, have a tendency to be both hysterical and corrupt. Enrico is neither. He is an ideal representative of the new face of Italy, while retaining the Italian capacity for creative thought. Enrico is more strategic and rational, and therefore more global-looking than his other predecessors.

We discussed the problem of Gazza, and Enrico had obviously thought long and hard about how to handle things. Although very annoyed that Gazza was in Paris as a kind of hostage, he knew that above all he had to protect the club. There was no point in losing his temper, the most important thing was to decide a strategy and stick to it. The prime objective was to get Gazza from Paris to Seville as quietly as possible. The press wouldn't be too much of a problem. It was Monday, so Gazza wouldn't be expected at the training ground, and as he had not played on the Sunday, they would be expecting him to be resting at the villa.

Enrico and I spoke to Mel Stein and we all agreed to have a meeting in Paris to discuss various aspects of the contract. Enrico had not been present for any of the negotiations concerning Paul, as he had only been at Lazio about a month, so

159

he had to confer with Director of Finance, Giancarlo Guerra. I was to come along to translate, and ensure things went smoothly.

We were staying near the Charles de Gaulle airport at the Hyatt Regency. The meeting started at nearly midnight and we spent hours discussing the various matters, most of which revolved around the fact that Paul still had not been paid after the Lazio–Totttenham friendly match in September. Enrico was very reasonable and agreed the outstanding points. He made it clear, though, that he did not wish to pay for anything that Lazio hadn't already agreed to. The club would, however, look into the possibility of arranging another friendly match, without committing themselves in any way. This seemed to satisfy Stein and Lazarus.

Eventually, by 5 am we had discussed everything. I got to bed at six, but an hour later the phone rang. It was Gazza, with a thousand questions. 'What time do the planes go from Paris to Rome? What time from Paris to London? And Paris to Seville? How can I cash money from my credit card as I have to leave some for Sheryl…?' and on it went. I phoned his hotel and explained that I had to get him to Spain in a couple of hours and could they give me a hand with some information. They couldn't cash money on his credit card, but there was a place just inside Eurodisney called Fantasyland, which had a cash machine. So at 7.20 am, I was on the phone to Gazza explaining how he could get to Fantasyland and what he had to do with his credit card. After one hour's sleep, I felt I could do with a trip to Fantasyland myself. In fact, the way things were going, we could have been there already.

Having arranged everything, I met Enrico and Giancarlo downstairs for breakfast, and we waited for Gazza to turn up. He had to come 60 kilometres in a taxi from Eurodisney. At 9.15, there was no sign of him, and Enrico was beginning to pace around. At 9.30, I called Sheryl who said he had left, but forgotten his passport so the hotel people had had to chase after him. Ten minutes later, he turned up and we charged off to Charles de Gaulle airport, hoping to make the 10 am flight. On arrival, we scanned the departure board, but couldn't find our flight. Very odd. We found the British Airways check-in desk and, after what seemed like an eternity, managed to gain the attention of a member of the ground staff. Staring at us as if we were two aliens from the planet Zorb, the young lady casually informed us that the flight to Seville was just about to take off – from Orly.

After recovering from this minor setback, Giancarlo took things in hand and strode off to see if there was another flight. He discovered there was a flight to Madrid at 10.40 am, with a connection to Seville, so we opted for that one. The check-in staff (finally) recognized Paul and he signed a few autographs. Once on board, I got him to sign the rest of the items I had to distribute to various charities, and then we took off. At last we could all relax. I was sitting next to Gazza, with Enrico and Giancarlo behind us. All went well for the first twenty minutes, but then a strange, continuous beeping noise was heard coming from the front of the aircraft. Gazza hated flying and as soon as he heard the noise, he flipped. Ashen-faced and gripping his seat tightly, he was convinced something was wrong. 'It's going to crash, it's going to crash,' he kept stammering, all the while looking round the plane with his eyes filled with fear. Eventually, we managed to calm him down. I told him to breathe deeply and close his eyes and, as no-one else had panicked, it was obvious we weren't going to crash. We poured a couple of mini bottles of champagne down him, ate lunch and, thankfully, he fell asleep. He still hadn't completely recovered from the 'flu and I hoped he was going to be all right to play. Judging by the look on Enrico's face, if it meant Gazza had to be frog-marched onto the pitch by his team-mates, he was going to play in Seville.

We arrived in Madrid, had lunch again, read the newspapers and then Gazza went for a wander. When it was time to board the plane for Seville, he still hadn't returned. 'Wouldn't it be funny if we lost him now,' I quipped. Enrico and

Giancarlo looked at me, unamused. I eventually found him ambling along the concourse. We made our short flight to Seville and by the time we arrived, Gazza was getting psyched up to meet Maradona. He had withdrawn into his own little world and was obviously concentrating on the match. It was a case of pride for him; he didn't want to meet the world's greatest player and be in his shadow. Both of them had colourful reputations off the pitch; it would be interesting to see who came out the winner.

The television cameras and journalists were waiting to meet us at the airport. One of the journalists commented that Maradona was all charged up and looking forward to *this* appointment. Gazza mistook him as saying Maradona was *dis*appointed.

'Why, has he been run over?' he asked cheekily.

We got to the team hotel and had time for a quick shower, and then it was off to the stadium. It was not very full, but I did meet up with a small posse of English journalists. Gazza came out and, once the match had started, put in a few nice touches. Maradona strolled about the pitch, hardly breaking into a run, but when he touched the ball it was magic. Nothing could take away that talent, he could do things with the ball that nobody else could, apart perhaps from Gazza.

[Diego Maradona had lived an erratic life style. He led Napoli to their glorious league championship, he inspired Argentina to be world champions in 1986, but he had also delved into the low life, allegedly getting involved in drugs and being seen in seedy nightclubs. It was a wonder that he could still thrill the crowd with his football genius.]

As half-time approached, Gazza was beginning to tire. He had already signalled to Zoff to take him off when, with only minutes on the clock, he picked up the ball about 40 yards from goal and went on a slalom run through the Seville defence, beating first one, then another, and then yet another player before calmly rounding goalkeeper Unzue to score. It was the pupil copying the master, and the stadium erupted.

As Gazza and Maradona met in midfield, the Argentinian shook his hand in admiration of Gazza's fine goal.

After the match at Seville airport, I had quite a long chat with Dino Zoff about Paul's level of fitness.

'He's not the same player he was a month ago,' said Zoff, with a worried frown on his face.

'Maybe it's the 'flu,' I ventured.

'Picking up the 'flu so quickly is just another indication of his general health. He seems to be out of sorts.'

Zoff was clearly concerned about Paul and had noticed the player wasn't as committed to training as he had been a few weeks before. I thought he was obviously finding himself torn between his need for Sheryl and his love of football. The Lazio coach knew that Gazza had to start leading a more regular life, or he would jeopardize his career. On our flight back to Rome, Gazza confessed that he couldn't remember much about the goal against Seville, as his legs had gone. But everyone assured him it had been a great goal.

Gazza was due to join the England party for the match against Turkey and he called me the next day to find out about his ticket. He was being very reliable as far as I was concerned – when he said he would ring he did, even when out shopping with Sheryl. I felt we had a really good relationship based on trust. He was quite happy with me talking to Lazio for him, and I was often the person he turned to when he needed minor problems sorting out. I had become the Mel Stein of Rome.

When Gazza's October pay packet arrived, he asked me how much was in it. When I told him, he shook his head in disbelief and smiled. I could see his mind had gone back to his Newcastle days when he had been an apprentice earning a pittance. Now he was in Rome earning a fortune, but perhaps it wasn't making him as happy as he thought it would.

Graham Taylor called me to ask about Gazza. I told him about the Eurodisney incident and that Paul still had a touch of 'flu, which meant he really shouldn't have been trailing round the shops with Sheryl. Graham just said, 'Make sure he gets on the plane to us, and we'll look after him this end.'

On the Saturday, Gazza's sister, Anna, was getting married and Gazza was to be best man. Graham Taylor had given him permission to attend, as long as he was back for Sunday morning training. The England manager had re-organized his entire schedule so that all the players would have Saturday as a free day, and Gazza wouldn't appear to have been given any special favours Lawrie McMenemy was going as well, and Gianni Zeqireya had been invited with his wife, to keep an eye on the security side.

However, things did not proceed smoothly as Sheryl refused to go to the wedding at the last minute. Graham Taylor had driven Paul down from Lilleshall to Burnham Beeches in his car, so he could have a chat to Gazza before he went to Newcastle. It had been arranged that he would meet Sheryl and they would go off together. They went to wait for Sheryl and Paul asked if he could have a brandy. Graham said, yes, and that he would join him. He thought he should show a bit of comradeship towards Gazza to make him feel at ease.

Five brandies later, Graham could hardly stand up. He told me later, 'I'm just not used to drinking that amount in such a short space of time on an empty stomach, I could hardly get back to the team hotel.'

I had a mental picture of Gazza staggering back to the hotel along a dark deserted road carrying the England manager on his shoulder! Needless to say, it was the last time Graham tried to keep Gazza company in the drinking stakes.

Sheryl turned up and announced that she wasn't going, so Gazza took off without her. The wedding was a great success. It had been a typical Geordie celebration with friends and family. Gazza took his best man duties seriously and told everyone what a beautiful sister he had – and that he was still up to his old jokes!

Even security man Gianni got into the spirit of things. As Lawrie McMenemy recalls, 'I was impressed with the security chap, he went all round the building checking entrances and exits, and making sure the guests were controlled. Later on in the evening, I went looking for him but couldn't find him. I peered into the main room and saw Gazza sitting quietly with his mates, and then suddenly noticed an amazing thing. The serious sober type of a few hours ago was up on stage, singing and dancing with the band. Gazza had done him!' (In fact, Gianni Zeqireya had his drinks spiked at the reception.)

Sheryl hadn't attended the wedding, despite reports in the press that she had been seen with Gazza and that the two had become engaged. Mel told me that there had been a 'massive row', I gathered that Sheryl and Paul's Mum had fallen out in a big way when Carol had told Sheryl what she thought of her.

Meanwhile at Wembley, Gazza was having his best match for England since his comeback. Against the Turks, England's tactic was to give Gazza the ball whenever possible and allow him the freedom to get forward from midfield to support the front-runners. Alan Shearer and Ian Wright were told to run wide, pulling the Turkish centre-backs out of position and thereby create space for Gazza to exploit. Behind him, Carlton Palmer and Paul Ince were instructed to keep things tight in midfield, while David Platt would be looking to make his usual late runs into the penalty area. The two full-backs, as well as performing their normal defensive duties, were encouraged to get down the wings and provide the width.

The plan worked well on the night and England won 4–0, with the star of the show, Gazza, scoring two goals. His determination had lifted the team and his skill on the ball had been matched by his ability to bring others into the game. Terry Venables commented: 'He was allowed freedom to play...in this situation, he becomes alive with the ball. I haven't seen him go as far forward in Italy, he rarely runs ahead of the ball.'

It was after this match that Graham Taylor uttered the prophetic words, 'Please God, don't let anything go wrong with Paul Gascoigne.' Taylor admitted, 'He [Paul] has still got something about him which, if we aren't steady, could bring him down. The feeling is always there and that's why we have to hope nothing goes wrong. I can only hope and believe that he is learning. I have been so impressed by him this season, but this is the first time I've ever got close to him.' Graham regretted that it would be nearly three months before England would play again. He had wanted the team to get together over Christmas, but the various club commitments would make this impossible.

Little did he know what was to come. Gazza won the Man of the Match award, two business-class tickets from American Airlines to fly to New York, but he put them back into the pot and let another team-mate win them as he said he hadn't been the best player. His team-mates loved him because he was so committed and so unselfish. He would always be the first to praise another player rather than take the glory himself.

Gazza flew back to Italy looking like a well-to-do business-man, dressed in a smart suit and reading the *Financial Times*. It was obvious the two England matches had buoyed up his confidence.

Meanwhile, the relationship between Paul and Sheryl had reached a watershed. In a telephone conversation with me on the Saturday night following the England victory over Turkey, and when Lazio were away preparing for next day's away match against Foggia, Sheryl admitted that things had been rough between them, and another fight had ensued. Her father, Richard, had become involved and Paul had ended up in tears on the phone to him. As Sheryl said, 'It was all out in the open now.'

Paul had said that nothing meant more to him than her, and Sheryl had made it clear that she would have nothing more to do with his family, in particular his mother. I said I thought this would put him under enormous pressure, but she was adamant. It was at this point that his relationship with his family was put under strain. Sheryl's influence over

Gazza was growing stronger by the day.

The following week it was the derby match, and the tension was starting to build. There was nothing like a Rome derby, it was the one match Lazio had to win. Ever since Gazza had been in Italy, the fans had said that they didn't care if he took a year to come back to full recovery – just so long as he helped Lazio beat arch rivals, Roma.

Gary and Michelle Lineker decided to come to the match, and arrived from London on the Sunday morning. Gazza was very wound up. The night before the match, the players had been paraded before the fans outside the hotel and they had impressed upon the team the importance of winning. We saw Gazza just before kick-off and he was very uptight, fidgeting nervously, with his eyes wandering madly.

The scenes inside the Olympic stadium were incredible, with more than 70,000 fans chanting and waiving flags. It was a cauldron of rivalry and excitement, the nearest thing to a modern-day Colosseum. As the teams were announced, the two sets of fans unfurled massive banners that stretched across almost the entire width of the terraces, and the Roma fans lit fireworks into the sky. Everyone was looking forward to a great match and to seeing the stars of both sides – Gazza, Winter and Signori for Lazio, Giannini and Haessler for Roma.

The match started off badly for Gazza's team, with Roma outplaying them for most of the first half. Four minutes into the second half, Roma's captain, Giannini, scored to put his side ahead. Up to this point, Gascoigne had been strangely quiet and ineffective. He seemed to have got swept up in the tension and appeared to be nervous and indecisive. Roma were looking good to break their usual run of draws and win the match. Then, in the 88th minute, a cross from the right wing flew into the Roma penalty area. Up leapt Gazza, from a crowd of players in the penalty area, to plant a perfect header past the Roma keeper into the back of the net. The Lazio fans erupted in joy. It was the perfect moment for the sleeping lion to awaken. He admitted after the match that before the goal, he had been worrying about how he would face the public in the streets of Rome if Lazio lost the derby. Now he had saved the day. Gazza ran towards the fans, tears streaming down his face, as the emotion of the day got to him. He continued to cry all the way to the dressing room. He had been transformed from insignificant bystander to hero, all in the space of a couple of minutes.

That evening, Gary, Michelle, their friends Dan and Laura and I, all went out to celebrate with Karlheinz Riedle, Thomas Doll, Aron Winter and their respective partners. Gazza had declined to come along as he had his family and friends around. He said he would see Gary and Michelle the next day for lunch.

Trying to get everyone sorted out that night was rather like being a member of the organizing committee to the United Nations. As we were sat round the table, Karlheinz Riedle had said he was a big fan of Gary's. He even had an English sheepdog named 'Gary'! Karlheinz and Gary are somewhat alike in character, both quiet and professional in their approach, and also very attached to their families. They even play in a similar striking role. All three Lazio players were interested in Gary's experiences in Japan, especially Karlheinz, who said he would like to finish his career there in a few year's time. The players were very impressed with Gary Lineker, as he was with them. It was an enjoyable evening, rounded off with a birthday cake for Gary and the singing of 'Happy Birthday', in three different languages!

The next day was Gary's actual birthday and we went out with Paul and Sheryl for lunch. Gazza took command, ordered the lunch and paid the bill. Gary and Gazza are poles apart, but have a common love of football, and Gary was particularly interested to hear how Gazza was getting on, and pleased to know that he liked the Italian way of life, and the football. Gary had played in Spain and so knew about the pressures. I got the distinct impression that Sheryl was envious of Gary and Michelle's calm and understanding relationship. It was obvious that they were a team, whereas Gazza and Sheryl were more competitive.

Bianca went into a clinic to have her adenoids out on the Tuesday after the derby, and Sheryl accompanied her and slept in the clinic. Paul was left to look after Mason in the villa. For some reason, Sheryl didn't want the babysitter, Marica, to look after Mason, as she said Marica was too lenient with the children, not making them go to bed on time, and allowing them to eat when they felt like it. She didn't want me to keep an eye on Mason either, so Paul had to take over.

It ended in a big song and dance with the club. Lazio were due to play a friendly match against Aquila, prior to a league match on the Sunday away to Pescara. For these games, the team would be leaving on the Thursday and not returning until the Sunday. Paul wanted to join them on the Friday, by which time Bianca would be out of the clinic, but Zoff needed him. As a compromise, Lazio allowed him to leave later than the rest of the team on the Thursday. It was ridiculous that Sheryl wouldn't leave either Marica or I in charge of Mason, when in the past she had gone off quite happily to England and left both children with us. In the end, she had to let Marica look after Mason, as Paul had to join the Lazio squad.

Bianca came out of the clinic with her mother on the Friday, and they went home to the villa. Sheryl was restless and wanted to go home to London for a few days. Paul was keen to her to stay until Lazio returned on the Sunday, then they could all go off for a couple of days. Zoff had said that if he played well, he could have a couple of days off and report back to training on the the Wednesday. Saturday arrived, and I trooped round a large commercial centre with Sheryl, the kids and my boyfriend Massimo, to try and keep her mind off going back to London. Pescara was an important match, and Paul had to keep his mind on the job and not be worried about what was happening at home.

The next day I spoke to Sheryl who said she was going back to London that afternoon. She'd spoken to Paul and had a row with him as he didn't seem to care about the problems at home. She refused to speak to him and left the answering machine on when he called. I called him in Pescara and he seemed quite calm. I then phoned Sheryl and said she really had to consider what pressure Paul was under as he was away from home and facing an important match. She said, 'Oh, you would see it from a footballing point of view,' and asked for the phone number of the team hotel, so she could call Paul.

The match against Pescara was important. The team had decided to go into press blackout to avoid external pressure and, as a result, they played a much better match than at the derby. Gazza was outstanding, making a decisive contribution to the game and scoring a spectacular goal in which he went past three Pescara defenders. Lazio went on to win 3-2, and Gazza's presence had made all the difference. Though he was substituted in the 81st minute after taking a blow on the left calf, his performance had earned him the right to join Sheryl in London. Here was proof that when he put his mind to it, in spite of all the other problems, he could still play a great game of football. It was a win that Lazio badly needed as it moved them up the league table and within sight of a place in Europe the following season.

He returned on the Tuesday afternoon having visited Father Christmas with the children and set in motion the preparations for Christmas. Mel and Len arrived in Rome on the 13 December to watch the Lazio-Inter match. Gascoigne didn't play in that one as the calf injury was still giving him a bit of trouble. Lazio were making unhappy noises as they felt he really should have stayed behind and had treatment on it and not gone charging off to London. His decision to stay at home and not join the team at the hotel, did not add to his popularity. The Italians were doing everything to make sure he had an easy passage. Lazio had been more than patient with him, but now if he didn't get to grips with things they would be forced to be a little less sympathetic.

Mel, Len and I had various meetings with the bank and with the merchandising people, and we had lunch with Massimo who was going to provide us with some sponsorship contacts with companies like Epson and Uniroyal. Afterwards we went in search of pirate merchandise as both Mel and Len, rightly so, wanted to protect the official Gazza merchandise.

As we headed towards Christmas, the team doctor told me that Paul was due to do an eight-day muscle reinforcement programme, which he should do over the Christmas break. Knowing that he wouldn't be thrilled to do it in Rome, we found a centre in London, the Harpenden Sports Injury Clinic and a doctor Colin Crosby to supervise things. When a sportsman has suffered as bad an injury as Gascoigne, he has to do special exercises every three or four months to ensure that the thigh muscles are strengthened to support the knee. Gazza thought this was a case of over-reacting and decided he'd do the exercises on his own, and visit John Sheridan to have the knee checked. Team doctor Bartolini wasn't happy about this, but Zoff decided to treat Gazza like an adult as it was up to him if he did the exercises. If he didn't do them he'd be the one to suffer. We all had a chat in the deserted dressing room and Zoff expressed his concern.

'Tell him he seems to have his mind on other things and that I've noticed he's not training like he used to.'

When I relayed these comments to Paul, he swept his hand through his hair and admitted to not concentrating, but that he didn't know why. He was frustrated at not playing again and doing exercises to help his calf injury. He had thrown his football boots out of the training ground into the building next door. But when he asked Maurizio Manzini to go and get them, Maurizio said he couldn't. The reason? Next door was the 'carabinieri', or military police and he would probably be shot if he wandered in without official permission!

Zoff said he understood there would be difficult moments

as he came back after a long injury and was forced to take things slowly. Showing calm intelligence, he went off to tell Gazza to have a good Christmas and come back fit and refreshed. So we got the office Christmas cards out, and I went home on the 19 December. Before I went Paul asked me to arrange a withdrawal of some money for Christmas.

Sheryl said she would ring me to let me know if she was free for a drink. She didn't and when I turned up at the airport the day after I arrived in England to make sure that they got their Ford car, which I'd arranged for them to have on free hire, she just said, 'What are you doing here?' I would have thought that she could have said 'Happy Christmas', but obviously she had decided that wasn't appropriate.

On Boxing Day, I had a call from the owner of the house to say that the villa had been burgled. Nothing had been taken except the £30,000 worth of new clothes that Paul had bought for himself and Sheryl.

Paul was due to go back to Rome on the Sunday after Christmas day. On the 30 December, Maurizio Manzini rang me to say that Paul was on his way to England. The official reason was that his father was ill in hospital, which he was, and that he had a slight thigh strain so wouldn't be able to play the following Sunday. The 'other' reason was that Sheryl had not travelled back to Rome with him and was showing no signs of wanting to return. Maurizio said he'd been in tears in the dressing room and they'd decided to send him home for a few days.

Mel, as is his forte, took over the situation without informing me, and his wife Marilyn arranged for Paul and Sheryl to meet and discuss their relationship. The next day Mel and Len went to Paul's house in Hoddesdon and met both Paul and Sheryl to try and sort things out. Apparently, Sheryl wanted Paul to take more interest in the things she liked doing like going to the theatre and concerts, Mel said she wasn't used to going out with a footballer.

Mel, when I challenged him, said to to me that he 'wasn't a

fan of Sheryl's'. But I was furious that Mel hadn't even informed me of this latest hiccup. As usual, I was just the uninformed parlour maid.

In the end, Sheryl was once more persuaded to return to Italy and Lazio started the New Year with a 3–0 win in the league, without our hero. If 1992 had been full of ups and downs, 1993 was to be even more unpredictable.

BELOW THE BELT

January 1993 was a difficult month for everyone. Gazza and Sheryl had come back to Rome together, and on 6 January, Lazio played in a mini tournament in the Olympic stadium. It was called Lazio Day, and was a tribute to Tommaso Maestrelli, the manager who had led the team to league championship victory nearly twenty years before. Mel and Len came down to Rome to try and sort things out with Paul, after the return to England debacle.

At this point I was still part of the group, even though neither Paul nor Sheryl had phoned me since they'd been back. I presumed this was because they were having problems in their relationship, and needed space to sort it all out. It was becoming increasingly obvious that Sheryl was not happy living in Rome. She appeared to want out, but on her terms.

Mel, Len and I went to the stadium where we met Enrico Bendoni. It was made clear at this meeting by Bendoni that Paul's behaviour would no longer be tolerated by the club, and he had to buckle down and think football. They were unhappy that he had gone home over the New Year, rather than stay with the team. It was time to sort out his personal problems and concentrate on football. At this point, I had to say that I agreed entirely with Lazio. Having lived through the Ian Rush experience with Juventus, I could see that Lazio had been more than patient with Gazza. They had allowed him to go home when he had needed to after Christmas, they had given him extra days so he could occasionally go back to London, and swallowed the Eurodisney debacle with only a mild telling off and a small fine. If it had been Juventus, or AC Milan, he would have been called into the chairman's office, either Boniperti's or Berlusconi's, told to get his act together, and if he didn't like it then he could go home and stay home. Both Juventus and AC Milan were of the opinion that no player was bigger than the club. Lazio were trying to build their team round one player – Gazza – and up to a point they were willing to accommodate his needs and help him settle into the Italian way of life, both on and off the pitch. Mel and Len were quite subdued and agreed that it wasn't the time to push things. They were all going to speak to Gazza after the match in my absence, as Mel felt Gazza would be embarrassed if he was told off in front of a woman.

Gazza played badly during the tournament, looking unfit and disorientated, and afterwards Mel and Len went out to dinner with him and Sheryl to discuss things. I wasn't invited and, although I was unaware of it, this was to be a pointer towards my eventual downfall.

Mel was considered to be the pivotal point round which everything revolved. In the meetings with Lazio he treated me as little more than interpreter, even though I was closer to events in Italy than he was, and had extensive experience of both the intricate world of Italian football and public relations. We used to row about how the media was handled, or not handled as the case might be, and he used to keep Gazza very close to his chest. I could, to a certain extent, understand that a lawyer's relationship with his client has to be confidential and there would have been meetings at which my presence would not have been acceptable. But there were other times when my presence would have been useful. After all, Mel and Len were the ones who negotiated my contract with me and had decided in the first place that I would have some important role to play in Rome.

After this meeting, Mel called me from Fuimicino airport the next day to say that he would be late back in London for the meeting I had set up for him with Basic Merchandising, as the plane they were on had experienced engine failure, and had to return to Rome. He also had something more to say.

'Keep away from Gazza for a while, he's at war with the world.'

'What do you mean?' I asked.

'Well, he's in one of his moods when he drinks too much and doesn't want to see anyone. And he really doesn't like you going to the training ground.'

'What?' I was astonished. 'He's the one who asked me to meet him at the training ground when I went to and fro from the bank!'

'You know what he's like. Must go.'

What actually was said at this meeting, I will never know. But I do know that shortly after that, things went rapidly downhill as far as my position was concerned. I bumped into Paul about a week later as he was getting some money out of a cashpoint on Corso Francia near the training ground. He was very friendly and we had a laugh about some press conjecture that he was getting married. The following weekend, Lazio played away to Naples. Gazza got injured when he received a sharp blow on his left side, which had left him breathless and unable to continue in the second half. He was taken for an X-ray, which showed there were no broken ribs, just bruising. Lazio lost the match 3–1 amid reports that Gazza would be on his way back to England at the end of the season. The *People* newspaper came out with back page headlines saying Lazio wanted to sell him and Stein had been involved in talks with Newcastle. This was hotly denied by Lazio managing director, Lionello Celon who said, 'It's totally false, Lazio bought Gascoigne to build a team round him, to compete with Milan. We're hardly going to undo everything!'

But the rumours were rife and obviously unsettling Gazza.

The next day I received a call from Mel Stein about a conversation he had with Paul.

'I was speaking to him in Naples and suddenly out of the blue – we were talking about something else at the time – he said, "Jane doesn't work for me any more, does she?" I told him you did, and that I thought we were going to discuss it all when we were next in Rome at the end of January.' It was the first I knew about this.

Mel went on, 'So I've had to tell you, I'm really sorry but he's insistent.'

'Why?' I asked. I had the right to know the reason, at the very least. Mel implied it was because Sheryl hated me and that she was behind the decision.

My head was spinning as I put the phone down. I didn't understand what I had done or said. It was a mystery. I was determined to find out what had gone wrong and obtain an explanation from Paul. A letter arrived in the post a week later.

Dear Jane,

Further to our telephone conversation, I am sorry to have had to be the bearer of bad tidings the past few days. As I confirmed to you, Paul does want us to give you formal notice which, under the terms of the PGP contract, is 3 months. Obviously, you have not yet signed the ESP contract but in all the circumstances that's a bit academic at the moment. Len and I did want to talk to you face to face before we did this, but Paul is most insistent on this point. Obviously we will talk when we come out on the 31st/1st.

In the interim period – notice or not – the marketing will, we hope, proceed as that is in everybody's interest. Paul, through his company, has no intention of not honouring the contract so let's just try and soldier on until we can meet.

Regards

Yours sincerely
M. A. Stein

I was surprised at this, as in all my dealings with Paul he never indicated that he no longer wanted me around. After my conversation with Mel and then this fax, all the indications seemed to point to Sheryl Kyle as the reason for my dismissal. I found this weird. Last year, she had involved me in sorting out many problems and had often talked to me about her difficulties with Paul and her feelings of isolation living in Rome. It hardly seemed the behaviour of someone who couldn't stand me, yet Mel had been insistent. He repeated the same thing to my mother when she rang him. 'It's that bloody woman,' he had said to her when she had told him she was disgusted at the way I had been treated.

Sheryl had once said she couldn't stand Jane Featherstone, Gazza's former PA in London, for no better reason than she kept phoning up and her voice got on her nerves. Sheryl had also said to me, 'Paul thinks Jane Featherstone was having an affair with Mel.' On hearing this, I nearly died laughing. Jane was twenty-two and happily engaged to her boyfriend. Mel was in his forties and happily married to Marilyn.

This whole situation left me in no-mans land. I was to see my notice out for three months, but what about the day-to-day dealings with Gazza? Was I not to have contact, or should I carry on? Mel Stein could not offer a satisfactory answer, so I had to make up my own rules. Stein said that he and Lazarus would be down at the end of the month to try and sort it out. I asked him to arrange a meeting between themselves, Paul and I so we could get to the bottom of the story, and then if he couldn't stand the sight of me, I would just quietly disappear. They agreed to try and set this up.

The next day I spoke to a member of Paul's family, who told me that the previous Thursday, he had a call from Paul at five in the morning. Paul and Sheryl had another of their rows, and he had told her to go. He said that he was thoroughly fed up with the whole situation.

The phone call had gone on for over two hours, and Paul had been in tears. The next day he spoke to this family member six or seven times and, apparently, Sheryl had said that she wasn't prepared to go until she was ready, but he could stay in the villa if he wanted to. This situation had continued to Naples, where Gazza's attitude had softened towards Sheryl as he felt sorry for her. By the time he returned after the match, she was staying.

Lawrie McMenemy arrived in Rome with his wife Anne as guests of Lazio to watch them play Juventus. He went along to the Hotel degli Aranci to talk to Paul, and all four of us met up for a drink afterwards. Like Lawrie, Anne comes from the North East and has learnt to cope well with the demands of being the 'other half' of a man involved in professional sport. Lawrie spent all afternoon trying to keep Gazza happy, especially bearing in mind the importance of the upcoming match, although it seemed doubtful as to whether he would play.

Dino Zoff had a tough problem – four foreign players, three places, and three important matches in a week against Juventus, Torino (in the quarter-final of the Italian Cup), and Sampdoria. It was a vital week which could help determine whether Lazio went into Europe, either through their league placing or by going on to win the Italian Cup. Thomas Doll was ineligible for the Cup match, and Gazza was not 100% fit from the injury he picked up the previous week in Naples. It seemed as if Zoff would play Doll against Juventus, and then save Gazza for the midweek Italian cup match. The only foreigner who was absolutely certain to play was Aron Winter. As he said, 'Italian football offers the strongest competition in the world, so you can see how good you are as every week you're playing against and with the best players in the world. That has made me a better player.' Learning the language was very important. Aron, who already spoke Dutch, English and German, studied Italian every day, and therefore understood the culture better. Paul tried to learn Italian, and the club provided him with a teacher who went to his house, but it was never consistent.

I went to the match with Lawrie and Anne, and we saw Gazza by the changing rooms, dressed in his smart Lazio blazer, with a bottle of wine by his side, even if there was no evidence to say he had been drinking from it. Liam Brady was also at the match as he had been invited down by Telemontecarlo to appear on their Galagoal programme and comment on the day's events.

We all went to our various seats, unaware that another storm was about to break. As Platt and Gascoigne walked to their seats in the VIP box, one dressed in the Juventus blazer and the other in the Lazio, they were pestered by a reporter looking for a comment. Both teams were in press blackout, and both players refused to be drawn into comment. The only difference was the way they refused. Platt, an English gentleman representing his Italian club, continued to decline politely. Gazza, on the other hand, wasn't one to be diplomatic, and simply belched into the microphone. Rai television decided to broadcast it during prime time, so millions of Italians were privy to seeing an Englishman belch whilst they were tucking into their spaghetti. It caused an uproar and totally took the press attention away from the match, which ended in a 1–1 draw. This was a shame, because the game had highlighted a more determined and skillful Lazio, even without Gascoigne.

The next day the whole of Italy was discussing the incident. Lazio were mortally embarrassed. Even the normally silent Zoff admitted that, 'It wasn't a good way to behave.' Chairman Sergio Cragnotti was furious. He called Enrico Bendoni and was short and to the point: Gascoigne would be fined and summoned to lunch on Wednesday, so that the chairman could explain what it meant to be a Lazio player, and how Gazza was expected to observe certain basic rules. It wasn't the fact that he did it, it was the fact that he disgraced the image of the club by reacting in this way while wearing the Lazio blazer, and thereby representing the club. It was quite unacceptable.

Cragnotti had already experienced Gazza's sense of humour when, one day at the training ground, when the 'royal' visit of Cragnotti, Celon, Penacchia, Governato and Bendoni appeared, Gazza trotted up to his chairman, grinned and said, 'Tua figlia, grande tetti', or 'Your daughter, big tits.' Amid embarrassed giggles, it was established that Gazza had met not the chairman's daughter, but his brother's, and the subject was quickly dropped. However, that incident had been different, it hadn't happened in front of the press.

Sergio Cragnotti was a man with a burning ambition to take Lazio to the top of the ladder. He wanted desperately to emulate AC Milan chairman, Silvio Berlusconi, and give the fans and the world a truly entertaining spectacle of first-class football as well as a club that would push back the frontiers of modern sport. He had all the personal ingredients to realize his dream. A brilliant financier with international experience, he had the intelligence, the contacts and the ability to make it happen. He had bought Gascoigne to lead the team, and also to attract worldwide interest in the club. He didn't need a yobbo as part of the deal.

I was in total agreement with Cragnotti and the way he handled things. He was open to discussing the whole Gascoigne problem, and I explained that Terry Venables had been like a second father to Gascoigne, and perhaps he needed that kind of relationship with someone here. Someone who would look after him and make sure he was heard. Cragnotti has a keen sense of humour and gave me a wry grin as he said, 'I don't have time to tuck Gascoigne up in bed and read him bedtime stories.' They all knew Gascoigne was important and he was the cornerstone of the club, from which they hoped to build a world beating team. Now it was all down to him.

The only person willing to defend Gascoigne was Mel Stein, who misread the situation and said 'The Italians don't have a sense of humour. If he'd done that in England everyone would have laughed and it would have ended there.' In fact the English press didn't think it was particularly funny. The *Independent* commented, 'In the highly paid world of Italian football, certain behaviour is not tolerated. Gazza has damaged the image of English football and that of the English.' It looked like it was something that was going to run and run.

But there was another problem that at the time no-one knew about. Sheryl had packed her bags and returned to England with Bianca and Mason and friends John and Wendy Clarke who had been staying with her in the villa. The decision had been a long time coming, but finally both Gazza and Sheryl had decided that she was not happy in Italy and it would be better if she went home. There was no particular episode to provoke it, just Sheryl's feeling of isolation in Rome. She knew it was his job and although she would been willing to give it a try in the beginning, her dislike of the football world had led to the constant arguments. They phoned Mel Stein on the Sunday night after the Juventus match, and discussed it.

The *Sun* came out the following Saturday with 'Gazza's Girl Duzza Runna', and at that stage, although a brave face was being put on things, it seemed as if the relationship was finally going to die. There was a big sigh of relief all round Rome and in certain houses in England. Whether through her fault or not, Sheryl had not always been a stable influence on Gazza or his football. She left with all the clothes and jewellery he had bought her over the last few months, which were quite considerable – a stunning gold and diamond necklace, diamond bracelets and other necklaces and watches, plus designer clothes.

John Paul King, Gazza's brother-in-law, and Carl, his brother, and a couple of friends, moved into the villa to keep Paul company. They had a real laugh and Gazza managed to totally relax. They played jokes on one another and told ghost stories, and Paul and Carl dropped fireworks down the chimney. There was a great atmosphere; it was him and his mates together, and finally things started to change.

After months of emotional upheaval, it finally seemed as if he had discovered some stability and serenity. That Thursday night's Cup match was important, not only for the team but also for Gazza – he was on a personal bonus if Lazio won the Italian Cup. Lazio had arranged insurance to cover this eventuality, and it would come into place after the match against Torino, as they felt that if they got through this round, they would have a good chance of winning.

That night, Gazza set the Olympic stadium alight. I have rarely seen one player make such a difference to a team. He was the leader, the man who urged his companions on and dictated the pace and style of the game. Egged on by the chant of the Lazio fans ('Gazza, give us a burp'), he proved his worth to Lazio. He had total command of midfield, and was impossible to pin down. The game was only 20 minutes old when Gazza's solo run down the right wing resulted in a cross for Riedle who barged into Torino goalkeeper Marchegiani as he tried to find a path towards goal. The ball fell kindly for Neri, who promptly scored his first goal for Lazio. After half an hour, Gazza was in the thick of things again, deceiving Fusi with a drop of the shoulders and a sudden burst of acceleration. In desperation, the defender grabbed hold of Gazza's legs and a penalty was awarded, which Signori took and scored. It was 2–0 to Lazio, but Gazza was not finished. He picked up the ball in midfield and proceeded to beat the entire Torino defence, only to miss by a whisper scoring what would have been a memorable goal. Torino were forced to substitute Gazza's marker, Venturin, who had been having a nightmare, with the tough Mussi.

Right on half-time, Torino pulled a goal back to make it 2–1. The second half was locked in stalemate. With ten minutes to go to the final whistle, Zoff replaced the tiring Gazza, who was nevertheless furious, and Lazio began to lose their grip on the match. A few minutes from the end, a disastrous defensive mix-up in the Lazio goalmouth let in Torino for the equalizer. From 2–0, Lazio had thrown it away, the final score being 2–2. Now it would be all the more harder to win away in Turin in two weeks time.

The next day the Italian papers were delirious in their praise of Gascoigne. 'Gazza Lord', 'You should apologize to him', 'Bewitched by Gazza', 'Gascoigne is a star', screamed the headlines. In four days he had gone from a failed star, to being the king of the castle. But then that's Italy, and he had put in a great performance. In his lunch with him the day before the match, Cragnotti had got exactly right the balance between telling him off and encouraging him, demonstrating once again that he was a chairman not only capable of buying the best, but also managing it.

The day after the Cup match, Gazza had arranged to speak to the *Sun*, an exclusive interview for which they paid a large sum. But Gazza wasn't in speaking mood and when the journalist and photographer went to talk to him, they were met by him and his mates and a few beers. When it became apparent that nothing was doing, they left. Editor Kelvin McKenzie had not been amused. It was another case where money to talk had proved disastrous. Gazza had experienced a hell of a week – belching, splitting with Sheryl, lunch with his chairman and a magic performance on the pitch. It was just too risky to push it further.

Lawrie and Anne McMenemy arrived to watch the Lazio–Sampdoria match, and Lawrie was dutifully dispatched to do a babysitting job with Gazza in the team hotel, while Anne and I went shopping. Gazza still hated the enforced overnight stays with the team when he was in Rome, and was always happy with visitors. His friends used to go and keep him company and had almost become part of the team, so much so that Maurizio Manzini had to have a word with Gazza to re-establish the lines of conduct. Gazza was back in close contact with Sheryl by this stage and talked of them buying a house together. Apparently, Mason had been ringing Gazza at the villa to ask where his 'Daddy' was.

Mel and Len arrived the next day and I picked them up

from the airport. We had a meeting with Enrico Bendoni to discuss a possible friendly match. Mel wanted to organize a tournament in England and Scotland with Celtic, Sheffield Wednesday and Newcastle. As I had already been in contact with Liam Brady to see whether Celtic would be interested, I was less than happy at Mel's attempts to cut me out of the situation. In any case, Liam spoke Italian and knew Enrico Bendoni so he hardly needed any of us to introduce him, and he made it clear that he would deal directly with Lazio. Mel and Len were talking to some of the Lazio players to see what deals they could do, and they were hoping to speak to Beppe Signori to see if they could represent him. I found the whole thing annoying.

After the match, I was supposed to meet with Mel, Len and Paul to discuss my situation, which was still very much on hold. Paul had an average game and was substituted during the second half. When Mel rang me up, he said that Paul was tired and in a bad mood and didn't want to discuss anything. They said they would just go out locally to eat. I later learnt that 18 people had gone out to dinner, but they hadn't the time to sort out my problems!

I had no idea as to who was behind my exclusion. It could have been an unwise remark from Mel or Len to either Paul and Sheryl, it could have been something I unknowingly said or did. Whatever it was, I was never given a proper explanation. Mel said I should take heart from the fact that Gazza asked me to ring his Dad. If that was supposed to be a deep sign of trust and faith, it was lost on me. I always got on with John and didn't see why things should change.

Mel, Len and I flew up to have a meeting with Basic Merchandising, a company I introduced to them to get the whole Gazza merchandising operation under control. They both succeeded in making me feel like the junior secretary let out of the office for the day. I was allowed to contribute very little to the discussion and after this felt distinctly depressed about the whole situation. It was unbelievable that not only had I been sacked for doing something that I had not been informed about, but here they were taking over the place. We had a brief pause just before darkness so Mel could say his afternoon prayers, which did not particularly impress the chairman of Basic, Marco Boglione. The situation I found myself in made me uneasy with all the Gascoigne group. Someone had stuck the knife in and I wanted to know who.

I returned to Rome later that week. January had all in all been a strange month. What would happen next? I didn't have long to find out.

Paul stalked out of the training ground and was fined for refusing to speak to Enrico Bendoni. Sheryl was due back in Rome to do an interview with Paul, about how happy they were, and how living apart had just made them closer. The *Sun* and *News International* were paying a substantial five-figure sum for the privilege of learning that Paul played Sooty and sweep games with the kids, and that he was ever so romantic.

I bumped into Paul in the bank and he certainly didn't seem as if he had a problem with me. He seemed slightly embarrassed, but was his usual friendly self when he realized I wasn't going to ignore him or bite his head off. I attempted to enquire what was up.

"I've got a lot of problems at the moment,' he said.

'Well you can come to me if you have a problem, don't forget that,' I replied. He thanked me and gave me a peck on the cheek.

Paul and Sheryl did their interviews with a battery of journalists, and then she left to go back to London. A local paparazzi tried to get photos and was almost attacked, an incident which ended up all over the papers. I went to see Enrico Bendoni as I felt that I was getting nowhere with Mel and Len, and that it was time Lazio knew about my situation. Enrico was not pleased to learn that I had been given the push, as he considered that I was an important element in the group. I understood Italian football, and I appreciated the difficulties that an English player could encounter in Italy. I also learnt that Lazio were effectively paying for me. Apart from Paul's contract, there was a smaller one for various ancilliary services, including the provision of an interpreter. I never understood if that was for me or what. Enrico promised to talk to Mel and Len, which he did through Maurizio Manzini who speaks English, but Mel insisted that Paul would not change his mind. Lazio were and always have been very supportive of me. It was not their problem, but they thought that I had been treated badly considering the good job I had done, and they did everything they could to try and get Mel to change the situation. But he said he couldn't, so that was that, and I decided to get on with my life, and not allow the mysterious surroundings of my departure to affect me too much.

Gazza had another cracking match away to Fiorentina, which Lazio won 2–0. It seemed as if they really were on their way to Europe. Once again, Gazza starred in midfield. But the next week, things came down to earth with a bump. Lazio were knocked out of the Italian Cup in the return match against Torino. Torino won 3–2, Gazza played badly, his team-mates were affected by his performance, and the result meant that Lazio had to finish high in the league table in order to qualify for Europe the following season.

England were due to play San Marino the following week. Would Graham Taylor's worries come true? Was something going to happen to Gascoigne?

Torino was the setting for the next Gazza headline story – the so-called farting incident. An Italian journalist had approached Gazza to ask him a couple of general questions and our well mannered diplomat replied in a rather unusual manner. I spoke to the Lazio employees who had been present, and they, much to their embarrassment, confirmed the incident. I spoke to Mel who had also been in the hotel meeting various people, and he denied that it was a breaking of wind, saying a journalist had heard his stomach rumble. Whatever the truth of the matter, it gained momentum in the press, although officially Lazio chose to ignore it, and eventually it just petered out.

The day before the home match against Cagliari, Steve Howard of the *Sun* interviewed Sergio Cragnotti. The chairman was relaxed and open. He still considered Paul Gascoigne to be an outstanding player, but he had to find the right balance between exuberance and professionalism. When asked if Gascoigne would be captain of the team, he smiled and said time would tell. Certainly at the moment, Lazio couldn't consider giving him the responsibility of being captain. He seemed concerned as to what was happening with Paul and his girlfriend. First they split up, then she was back on the scene. It seemed confusing for everyone, not least of all, Gazza, and Cragnotti didn't want his players to have unnecessary complications in their lives.

Lazio had an awful match against Cagliari and lost 2–1. It was an unexpected result, and mostly the blame fell on a truly appalling Lazio defence, although no-one played particularly well. Sheryl and Mason flew down to Rome for the day, so that they could spend St Valentine's day with Paul, and they then got on a plane with him and flew back to London, along with his sister and brother-in-law. He then disappeared off into the night. Michelle Rogers, International Secretary of the English FA, rang me to find out if I had heard from him. I said I presumed he had gone off with Sheryl. The FA sent an official car to meet him, but he sent it to Newcastle with his friends in it! Finally, at 1.40 am, he turned up at Burnham Beeches, and joined the rest of the England team.

In fact, Gazza was in and out of the England camp during the few days they had together. San Marino weren't expected to be much opposition, but England couldn't afford to score a small number of goals, or they would be ridiculed by everyone. Besides, a high score was important in the event of a tie for a World Cup place and goal averages coming into play. In the event, it was a very one-sided match. David Platt was the hero, scoring four goals, but Gazza was a mere shadow of his former self. He returned to Italy on the Friday with a dose of 'flu, which, according to Mel Stein in an exclusive interview with Harry Harris of the *Daily Mirror*, he had on the night he played. Graham Taylor was furious as it made the England team manager and the team doctor look like a bunch of idiots. I was meant to see Mel Stein a few days later in London to sort out my situation, but he had caught 'flu from Paul and Sheryl, who he had seen after the England match. It did cross my mind that if he saw them then, why hadn't he found out what the problem was with me?

A very sad event happened on Ash Wednesday. England's 1966 World Cup captain and true ambassador of the game, Bobby Moore, died after a long battle against cancer, leaving a devastated widow, Stephanie, and two grown up children, Roberta and Dean. It shocked the football world, both at home and abroad. A real gentleman, Bobby had been much loved and admired. I wondered if Gazza would ever be like him. Bobby had genuine style and grace. Just before it was known that he had only a short time to live, he called me as he did all his friends, to say goodbye, without us knowing that we were talking to a dying man. He was the kind of human being who would touch your heart with kindness, and move you with his humility and modesty. There were very few men, in any walk of life, like Bobby Moore. I hoped Gazza and companions would follow his example.

On Saturday 27 February, exactly a year after we had been in Rome to watch the derby, I drove down to the capital with John Gascoigne, and his two mates, Mick and Jimmy. It was a pleasant journey. John had a new Land Rover discovery, which had been a present from Paul, and we cruised down the motorway having a laugh and a joke. The Geordies have a knack of making fun out of life, and Paul had caught this, although he had learnt that not everyone understood the

Geordie sense of humour. All three men remembered Paul when he was a lad and delivering papers. They would have all known it was him at the door as they heard the thump, thump as he continued to kick a football while doing his round. The conversation turned to his future and they all hoped he would find happiness. There had been a universal liking of ex-girl-friend Donna. Mick said what a great girl she'd been, very low-key, not at all pushy. Although they didn't openly say it, there was a great deal of concern. The once bubbly, open lad had turned into a more cautious, closed person. Whereas once Paul's family meant everything to him, now he spent most of his time with Sheryl and her children. The ties with the family were loosening, he was drifting away to a different life, a life that was full of uncertainty, and that was reflected in his football. One week brilliant, one week awful. Everyone, hoped that the inconsistency was due to the injury and the long layoff from playing football, but he seemed to be strug-gling with his physical fitness, and nowhere had this been more apparent than during the San Marino game.

We arrived at the villa and found Carol Gascoigne, and daughters Anna and Lindsay with respective husband and boyfriend. Carl had stayed behind in Newcastle to look after the animals. There was a shortage of pillows so Massimo and I went out to buy some, get muscle-soothing cream for Lindsay's sore back, painkillers for Mick's headache and a present of a set of spanners for John, so he could fix the car radio. When I got back, I found a large box of Milk tray choco-lates sitting by my car, as a thank you. The Newcastle family were a rock, a set of down-to-earth kind people, who knew Paul and provided him with consistency and security. But as he'd moved into a different world, so he'd moved away from them. The only constant was Mason, who Paul adored. Sheryl was determined that nothing would come between Paul and Mason. Ex-husband, Colin now had access to see his daugh-ter, Bianca, but he couldn't see his son, and Sheryl was fight-ing tooth and nail to prevent him from seeing Mason. The case has gone to the welfare officers, to see if some agreement could be reached, but it was a very difficult and awkward situation. How could Bianca see her real father and Mason not? As he got older and asked his sister who she had been to see, what would she say?

On 28 February, *La Gazzetta dello Sport* ran a big article quoting the referees as saying what a joy Gascoigne was to have on the pitch. Angelo Amendolia said, 'He's a person who reacts instinctively but he's never underhand.' Amendolia was also the referee for the Cup match against Torino in Turin. He says, 'At a certain point, about half an hour into the second half he said to me, "I'm gone, I can't play on, you play for me, you'll do better." So I said, "Will you referee?" He replied, "I haven't even got the energy to blow the whistle." Then he was substituted.'

Referee Roberto Bettin gave him some chewing gum when Gazza protested about a foul. 'It shut him up,' says Bettin. Carlo Squizzato says, 'You can see he's good natured and he always underplays fouls on him even though he risks more than most after his knee injury.'

Graziano Cesari, who refereed the Fiorentina–Lazio match, says after Gazza had been involved in the build-up to a Lazio goal, he went up to him and said, 'You're a champion!' and Gazza replied, 'You're the best referee in the world!'

'He was great on the pitch,' says Cesari.

That afternoon in the away match against Genoa, Gazza was sent off for reacting to a foul on him by Bortolazzi, the player who had nearly taken his leg off in his first match. But Gazza wasn't to be sent off normally. Like a true English gentleman, he shook everyone's hand and strode off to a hero's welcome. They all thought he had behaved very well, and the result was he was only given a one-match suspension, so he wouldn't miss the home match against Milan. In fact, if Gazza's off the pitch antics were somewhat unconventional, his behaviour on the pitch was always impeccable.

On the 1 March, I spoke to Mel Stein who was in a very conciliatory mood, and wanted to know what it was like down in Rome. The next day, I had an enlightening conversation with Graham Taylor, who was getting to the end of his tether with the Gascoigne problem. Taylor had tried to give Paul friendship and support, now it was coming back in his face. The San Marino match had been a disaster for Gascoigne and the stay in the team hotel even worse.

'Sometimes you talk to Gascoigne,' said Graham, 'and you don't know if he's taking it in or not. Sometimes you wonder if he cares what you're saying.'

Graham had asked Gazza about me, and Gazza just said dismissively that I was off in a month. His physical condition was awful.

'Last August/September he had been fighting to get fit and had been a harder, sleeker, fitter player, now he seemed uninterested and flabby, and it seemed to be down to the booze. In the days leading up to the match, he was drinking a lot of brandy. I shouldn't really have played him at all, but it's difficult to drop Gascoigne quietly.'

Taylor was in a quandary, should he stick behind him and help him to pull through, or should he drop him. I asked Graham why he thought Gascoigne drank.

'The sad thing is, I think he does it because he simply can't stop.' It was getting out of control, we all thought he needed help.

It all seemed to be falling apart. Graham was upset that such a great talent was going to waste.

'I can't carry Gascoigne, and if I drop him, I'll have to say why,' Graham said, almost prophetically. 'It's a hell of a situation. I feel for the lad, but I can't do anything. I have a World Cup to qualify for.' Taylor sounded depressed about the situation.

Back on the pitch, Lazio travelled to Parma and lost 2–1, Gazza flew to London to see Sheryl, as he was sitting out the match due to the one-match suspension. Lazio let him go, but they would have preferred it if he had decided to stay with the team, even if he could only give moral support. The following week was the big match, Milan against Lazio. The press billed it as Gazza against Baresi, 'the genius against the naughty genius'.

On the Friday before the match, Sheryl arrived and I decided finally to tackle her about why she disliked me. I was fed up with being told she hated me without a motive being given. I was told that on a plane journey, she reputedly had said to *Sun* photographer, Richard Pelham, 'You're a traitor, you went out to dinner with Jane.' It was back to the upper fourth mentality. I rang her at the Hassler hotel, where she was staying with Mason. She had refused to stay in the villa as Paul's family were there. She said it was like a Newcastle camp, and when Mason had asked why they couldn't go to the villa, she had said because the Newcastle relatives are there. She was going to the match, but wouldn't be sitting near Paul's Mum. Gianni Zeqireya was having to organize taking them all to the match, and arranging it so that Sheryl didn't bump into Paul's Mum.

Just to confuse the situation, she insisted that she had nothing against me.

'I have no problems with you,' she claimed. I explained that Mel had told me that the reason I was dismissed was because she hated me.

'Oh, that's typical of men. It's Paul's fault, he says one thing to one person, then something different to someone else. I found out he had been telling his Tottenham mates he had thrown me out, then at the same time he's on the phone begging me to come out and see him.'

Could it have been that Sheryl was instrumental in my dismissal? Sherl had always been a strong and dominant influence on Gazza. The only thing she said was that he went everywhere with Gianni, who did things for him free, the implication being why did he need me when he had someone who ran around for him and did things for free. When I told Lazio this, they were surprised as they understood immedi-

193

ately that my job and Gianni's position were completely different.

We all knew that it wouldn't be very long before she demanded to know what Mel and Len were up to, which is where the real decision making lay.

Lazio were off on a trip to Japan, to promote the image of the club and that of Gascoigne. They had signed up for a couple of friendly matches at the beginning of May, one with Grampus Eight, Gary Lineker's new team. Sheryl said that she was going as well, and looking forward to seeing Japan as she had never been there before.

I went to the training ground and saw Paul's family *en masse*, and eventually Sheryl when she turned up to collect Mason, who had been at the training ground with Paul. Gazza was a bit nervous when he saw me and when Sheryl arrived he seemed very agitated by my presence, which told me that she had something to do with my departure, even if she insisted otherwise. He was pacing up and down in the car park, with Mason running around beside him. His family were chatting to each other as Sheryl arrived in a taxi. Considering that Gazza did not like mixing women with football, it seemed odd that Sheryl had turned up at the training ground, especially as all the Lazio players were sitting in the team coach, waiting for Gazza to stop talking with Sheryl so they could go to the team hotel. You couldn't have had a more public place to have a discussion, especially with all the journalists lined up just outside the car park. Eventually, Maurizio Manzini called Paul to the coach and he departed with the rest of the team, while Sheryl took her Toyota Celica to the hotel.

John Paul King and John Coberman, the latter a long standing friend of Paul's from Tottenham days, decided to come with me to shop in one of the main shopping centres just outside the centre of Rome. They were both pretty fed up up with the petty arguments that were going on when one family was under one roof. As well as the immediate family,

Carol's younger brother Ian was there along with a cousin, Cyril, and one of the young Tottenham players. Uncle Ian had managed to have his throat cut in some violent northern argument and had recently reappeared on the scene, and had been given an expensive diamond ring by his favourite nephew, who he said was like a brother. There were arguments over who would sleep upstairs in Paul's bed. Uncle Ian reckoned it should be him, the rest of them reckoned it should be John and Anna. John and Anna got the vote, which was right, considering Anna was now pregnant again. It was a bit like *Goldilocks and the Three Bears*, with the only difference that Goldilocks was holed up in one of the best hotels in town, leaving the three bears to slug it out in the luxurious but prison-like villa. At this stage, it looked as if the three bears would all fall out and start fighting. It was getting so bad that shortly, no doubt, they would be arguing over who should eat the porridge! It was sad as his family are the most important factor in his life.

Paul was in a dilemma. That was how much he had changed. Old friends seemed to be dropped by the wayside as he embraced the new life. Mates like John Paul King and John Coberman had been around to listen to his heartfelt pleas in the middle of the night, or fetch and carry him here, there and everywhere whenever he clicked his fingers. John Paul has always remained a loyal and committed friend, rather than just a brother-in-law. He was one of the few people outside his immediate family, who would never give up on Paul, and would always be there when he needed him.

There were certain members of his family who were losing sleep over the Sheryl case. They knew she had a strong hold over him, which was not having an entirely positive effect, but they thought that if she chucked him, he might commit suicide out of sheer desperation. He's totally bowled over by her.

We all had a few hours break in the shopping centre, John Paul bought a little all-in-one outfit for his baby, and John Coberman wandered about looking like Kojak, the result of a

Gazza joke, when Gazza had shaved his hair and eyebrows in a wild moment at the villa.

Lazio versus Milan was one of the main matches of the day. I arrived at the Olympic stadium with Tottenham Director, Jonathan Crystal and a girlfriend of his, Dion. Jonathan, a great friend of Terry Venables, was a barrister famed for his work with clients Richard Branson and Jason Donovan. We bumped into Sheryl who was installed in her usual room near the dressing room. Sheryl had never gone unnoticed in the way she dressed and today she was obviously going through her cowgirl phase. Dressed in a pair of gold-studded, brown cowboy boots, dark brown tights, a micro brown suede skirt and matching fringed jacket, she looked like an extra from a spaghetti western. I refrained from asking where Trigger was!

Almost 70,000 fans had crowded into the magnificent Olympic stadium to see a great spectacle and they weren't disappointed, even though it always seemed as if the league champions in-waiting would be the winners. After nine minutes, Jean-Pierre Papin scored for Milan, followed by an own goal by Aron Winter in the 37th minute, which made it 2–0 to the league leaders. It would take Gazza to get Lazio out of this mess, and one minute later he scored from a position where many claimed he was in 'passive offside'. Either way, he was free of any markers and deftly put the ball in the back of the net, to the roar of the Lazio fans. In the second half, Milan seemed to lose concentration. Papin was substituted and in the 86th minute, Bergodi threw himself at the ball and scored to make it 2–2. Gazza had played a decent match, providing most of the more imaginative play, particularly in the first half, when once more his contribution in midfield had been decisive in keeping his side in the game.

The day after the match, Gazza took Sheryl and Mason to Fregene, one of the 'in-beaches', for lunch. It ended in an argument, when Gazza launched a bottle of mineral water at a photographer, who had been lying in wait outside. Meanwhile, I spoke to Mel who again assured me that the problem I had with Gazza was due to Sheryl, even after I told him about the conversation I'd had with her before the match. He said quite bluntly, 'Who do you want to believe, her or me?' He was concerned about the fact that Sheryl was off to Japan, and wanted to know why she was going. The whole matter of my dismissal was unsavoury and confusing.

On the Wednesday, John, Carol and Anna went to the weekly audience held by the Pope at St Peter's. They had front row seats organized by Gianni Zeqireya, as he had contact with a cardinal who was one of the Pope's right-hand men. It was one of the highlights of John and Carol's visit. Meeting the Pope was an emotional and thrilling moment. First they were taken up to the cardinal's office, where he had put a photo of Paul into one of the frames holding a picture of his holiness, the Pope. It was difficult to decide who had more influence in Rome! They were given cultured pearl rosaries and then taken to their seats to meet the man. Carol was still totally enamoured by the experience when I popped into the villa the following Saturday to find her sweeping out the kitchen (which judging by the number of people sweeping it out, was the cleanest floor in Rome), and looking at the photos she had of the event. It had been an experience that they would never forget, and one of the highlights of all the things that had happened to them since they had a superstar in the family. Dad John was in the garden digging out an allotment in the huge garden. He wanted to plant some vegetables for the family to eat when they stayed at the villa. I wasn't sure what the owner would say, but as we weren't sure he was the owner, it didn't seem to matter. In fact, the sale of the villa was still under discussion and, so it looked as if Paul wouldn't lose his year's rent.

Lazio away to Atalanta was another one of Gazza's better matches. 'Lazio made in Gascoigne' screamed the headline from *Il Corriere dello Sport*. It was a very good match for him, and it followed a series of positive performances. It seemed as if the real Gazza was emerging from the injury problems and off the-pitch anxieties. He had managed to juggle the family and Sheryl, keeping them both apart whilst seeing them all, and this was obviously giving him peace of mind to concentrate on his football. The match ended in a 2–2 draw, with a superb headed goal by Gascoigne in the 29th minute, but his overall contribution to the team had been much more important. Once again, he had been the leader in pushing Lazio to a good performance. According to one Atalanta fan, 'Gazza is a great player, far too good for Lazio'. At the end of the match the Atalanta fans, who come from Bergamo, deep in the north of Italy and are not noted for their impartiality, applauded Gascoigne as he left the pitch. They knew a champion when they saw one, and were willing to pay homage to him.

Team doctor Claudio Bartolini warned that Gascoigne still wasn't quite a hundred per cent fit. 'He's almost a hundred per cent fit, but not quite. He's had the normal ups and downs we expected from a player who has experienced as bad an injury as his. Now he has shown the kind of continuity that demonstrates he's almost back to peak fitness.'

If Lazio had experienced doubts about his character, they were now convinced that they had a champion, who would take the team to the top. Cragnotti warned any other club to forget about making offers for Gascoigne. He was 'untouchable'; even the normally reserved Zoff admitted that 'Although the team is good, Gascoigne is Gascoigne.'

The next day Gazza was guest of honour at a dinner to celebrate the formation of a fan club in his name. He was presented with an award, a plaque that he kissed and raised to the ceiling, and was given a hero's reception by all. The journalists had given him a lemon award for his difficult relationship with the press, but he would be unable to pick it up. He had another important date with the England national team for the World Cup qualifier against Turkey, in Izmir.

While Gazza was away from the Italian scene, Lazio got nearer to their dream of qualifying for Europe with a decisive 4–0 win against Udinese. Signori once again proved his worth with two goals, while Thomas Doll and Karlheinz Riedle were the other goalscorers.

Gazza's great performances couldn't last. England won 2–0 in Izmir with Gazza scoring the second goal, but that was the beginning of his decidedly off-form period. When he got back to Italy, Sheryl brought the children over to stay for Easter. John Gascoigne was staying at the villa, and he got out just before she arrived.

The next two games were appalling for Gazza. On 4 April, Lazio played away to Torino, and in a very mediocre match, Gascoigne was substituted in the second half. A week later it was a visit by Foggia, and he was again substituted at the beginning of the second half. These were two of his worst performances of the season, and they coincided with more press rumours that Paul and Sheryl were back arguing. Paul had even been sighted in Rome on his own.

The derby match was approaching and in spite of the problems in his private life, Paul showed a kind heart when a young fan, Jamie Hart, who was suffering from brain and spine tumours, arrived in Rome to see him. He spent time with him, chatting and giving him all sorts of mementos, including his boots. Maurizio Manzini was also very good and provided a signed shirt for the boy. The whole things was co-ordinated by my boyfriend Massimo, who found a different story when he went to Lazio to obtain tickets for the derby match for Jamie and his family, who were in Rome with him. The Lazio marketing manager said, dismissively, that it wasn't a marketing operation that interested the club, and neither he nor the club secretary could offer any solutions to the ticket problem.

Having received a negative response from Lazio, Massimo went to his old friends at Uniroyal, the tyre company, and the director, Antonio Andreucci was only too pleased to help out. He bought tickets and sent Jamie a letter saying that he hoped these tickets would help him to enjoy his stay in Rome and that Uniroyal were right behind him in his fight to live. It was a thoughtful and humane gesture and it touched the hearts of Jamie and his family.

By the time I got back from Dallas and London, I found the Lazio managers once more crying into their spaghetti. Only a month before everything had seemed to be getting better. Now the unpredictability of Gazza had once again taken over. Everyone was in for a bumpy ride.

I returned to Rome to find Gazza's telephone had been cut off – as he had forgotten to pay the bill and he was overdrawn at the bank. As nobody was looking after the day to day running of his affairs, they had got into a mess. Apart from that, his level of fitness wasn't wonderful and his general financial affairs were unclear. Mel had sent me a copy of the Basic Merchandising contract, but nothing had moved from that point. They were launching a Gazza line of various items of clothing, specifically aimed at the Japanese market. I only found this out by chance, having not been informed by Paul's 'advisers'. Mel had liaised with Paul over choosing which items he would be wearing to promote the line, and was not informed of any details. As Basic had been my contact, it would have been logical to involve me in the actual implementation of the contract. It might have improved my relationship with Gazza. It was at that point that I washed my hands of the whole affair. Having scrambled about the place trying to raise interest for companies to do publicity with Gazza, I had since my departure from the group, been asked by several companies if it would be possible to discuss publicity campaigns using Gazza. My stock reply was that they should contact Mel Stein. I wanted to make money for Gazza, but the whole situation was too fraught with problems.

I found Lazio concerned about the Gazza situation, especially his constant chaotic lifestyle which just wasn't conducive to that of a professional footballer in Italy. They had been extremely patient and understanding, but the love affair between Lazio and Paul Gascoigne seemed to have been slightly tarnished, although the fans in the main were still behind him. All they were hoping for was to see more consistent performances. Both Gazza and Winter missed the next league match, as they were called into their respective national teams for the World Cup qualifying match between England and Holland. Lazio were at home to Pescara, and won 2–1, even though it wasn't a great match. Cragnotti made a point of saying how much they had missed Winter.

In England, our wayward superstar was having problems with his knee. He insisted that he had received a blow to it during the derby match, but Lazio knew nothing of this, and as far as they were concerned had sent him as fit as a fiddle to England. The England camp said he had arrived with a slight injury. It turned out not to be serious, but if it had been it would have been an insurance man's nightmare. Lazio insisted he left them fit, England said he arrived injured. After a couple of days, the sore knee cleared up (luckily, the relationship between England and Lazio had not been damaged) and he was ready for the Holland match.

This was one of the key matches of England's qualifying group. England and Holland were the favourites to go through to the States, but tiny Norway had stolen a march on the two and were leading the group. There was also Poland, lurking behind, with games in hand. The first half went quite well, with Gascoigne, although not as prominent as usual, contributing to the game with his ability to control the ball and direct the pace of the game. England had taken the lead early on with a glorious strike from a free-kick by John Barnes, and Holland were on the rack when David Platt scored to make it 2–0. The Dutch, however, came back strongly and Bergkamp lobbed a splendid goal to bring it back to 2–1. Just before half-time Gazza was challenged by Wouters for a high ball and the Dutchman's elbow seemed to catch Gazza on the side of his head. This was to be the turning point of the game, Gazza didn't come out for the second half,

England lost control and allowed the Dutch to equalize from a penalty to make the final score 2–2. Next day, Gazza's injury was diagnosed as a depressed fracture of the left cheekbone, and he had to have an operation. This put paid to his trip to Japan. It also caused a lot of problems for Lazio, as Gascoigne had been an important element in the Far East Matches. Gascoigne had told Platt and Walker that he hadn't wanted to go, and now that he was injured he didn't have to. Aron Winter flew out of London with assistant manager Giancarlo Oddi, to Japan. Gascoigne remained in London and was operated on in a clinic in Essex. He recovered rapidly and was out at Thorpe Park with Sheryl and the children over the weekend.

John Coberman, meanwhile, was at the end of another Gazza joke. John, a good-natured type, was always suffering through Gazza's jokes. He was once spotted clinging precariously onto the ladder of a camper van as Gazza drove it round trying to shake him off. It was like the Benny Hill comedy show.

On Sunday 2 May, the *Sunday Mirror* published a front page article referring to my exit from the Gazza entourage, and what I thought of Sheryl. One of the first people to ring me was Mel Stein, who said that the article had damaged my reputation and it looked as if I had sold my story. He said that Sheryl had said that John and Carol would be pleased about it. However, he was more subdued than usual and admitted to me, 'I can understand, I've made mistakes as well.' He was referring to an extract that had appeared in the same newspaper from an article he wrote for the magazine, *Football Management*. In it, he criticized the world of football agents and managers, pointing out the amount of corruption that was going on, in his view, in terms of the number of backhanders paid to football managers in transfer deals. According to Mel, certain managers regularly took money from transfer deals, and players were better off dealing with solicitors such as him who worked on a fee only basis.

The football managers and agents who worked with the

players were, far from happy about these statements and wanted an apology.

At about this time, Mel Stein was to become increasingly pre-occupied with his own affairs after he was charged in the stat of Louisiana with conspiring to commit mail fraud and money laundering.

It was alleged that he had been involved with a character called Carlos Miro, the founder of Anglo American (an insurance company which collapsed in March of 1989, leaving $28 million in unpaid claims. Mel Stein denied any liability, promised to defend the action and the whole affair took up a large amount of his time.

The State of Louisiana sent out a news release from the Department of Insurance on 29 April 1993. The headline was 'British Lawyer named in Insurance Department Civil Suit, indicted on Federal Charges'. It went on to say:

'Commissioner Brown is continuing to pursue the civil claim in England against Stein and some of his partners who practised at Finers. In that suit Brown contends that through the use of the Finers client account, Stein and Finers assisted Miro in dishonest and fraudulent actions.

'Carlos Miro could not have done what he did without some help,' Commissioner Brown said, 'and whether it was specific advice or someone turning their head and looking the other way that allowed him to get away with this really doesn't matter. The bottom line is that other people either participated in making this happen, or considering the information they had available, they could have done something to prevent this and did not. Either way we are going to hold these people accountable.'

Stein collapsed under the strain and was admitted to the Grovelands Clinic in North London where he began treatment for a nervous breakdown.

This whole affair has left Gazza's affairs somewhat in the air. Since Mel has been out of circulation, no-one has really taken control. Not only has no-one tied up all the loose ends relating to my contract, but Gazza's day to day things have been neglected. In Italy he had to complete a form for the fiscal authorities, and Lazio called his lawyer, Carla Vissat, to enquire as to who they should send the relevant form to. She called London and London called me in spite of the fact they had consulted with Coopers of Lybrand regarding his internal financial affairs.

Sheryl called me after the *Sunday Mirror* article appeared, and insisted she had nothing to do with my dismissal.

'How are you?' I asked.

'How do you think I am after that article? Why did you do it?'

'Because Mel told me you hated me, and I'm fed up with being told you're the cause of my problems.'

Sheryl paused. 'It wasn't me,' she said, 'I told you when you rang me in Rome.'

'Yes, and I rang Mel and he told me I could believe him or believe you.'

'I've already argued with Paul about it, and told him he should have told you to your face. And we're seeing Mel this afternoon so I'll have it out with him as well.' I could hear Paul muttering in the background.

'Paul should have had the courage to tell me to my face,' I stated.

One of the reasons he didn't want you working for him was,' she lowered her voice, 'he said you were going to bed with the other players.'

I couldn't believe what I was hearing. It was pathetic. 'I haven't been having group sex with all the players in one go,' I said sarcastically.

Sheryl turned on the tears. 'I could lose Mason through this, how could you say the things you did?'

'I don't think you're a bad mother. I just pointed out what happened. Anyway, you won't lose Mason.'

'Oh, you're suddenly the welfare officer, are you? I have to see them this week and if they mention this, you'll know what *real* hurt is.'

I repeated that I didn't think she was a bad mother and Paul came on the phone, spitting and raging.

'You used the name Paul Gascoigne, you've been spending too much money from the promotions. How much money have you made for me?'

'I bought in Basic,' I said firmly. 'Anyway, if you have problems about how much I was earning go ask Len, he's the one who dealt with that side of things.'

It was an indication of just how badly managed the whole affair had been. I didn't see why I should be used as a scapegoat. Paul and I ended our conversation on bad terms, with him threatening to have me banned from the training ground and stadium, and anywhere else he felt like.

I rang Paul's Mum and Dad who were delighted by the article. 'You didn't say enough,' was Carol's comment, 'fancy leaving the bairns in a foreign country.' When I told her about his comments regarding money, she just said, 'Oh yes, he's angry because the Promotions company has gone bust.'

I felt sure custody of Mason hadn't been the real issue, and my thoughts were confirmed when I spoke to Colin the next day at an his estate agent's in Hertford. He assured me he was going for access to see his son, not custody. 'I live in a two bedroom flat now,' he said, 'how could I keep him? I just want to see my son.'

Graham Taylor rang me on Wednesday 5 May and we had a chat. He had obviously known I was leaving from the moment that I'd been given notice. As I had worked closely with him, there was little point in hiding it. He said that he'd received a letter from Lazio, saying that they'd release Paul for the two World Cup qualifying matches, but not for the friendly tournament in the States at the beginning of June, as they needed the player for their own end of season friendly matches. Graham understood this and said it was no problem. Finally, they'd asked for the England team's plans for 1993/94. Graham had built up an extremely good relationship with Lazio and he was keen that it should continue, especially bearing in mind the special temperament of the player concerned.

Gazza returned to Italy on the 6 May, and seemed a different person. Intuitive if not academic, he had understood that he'd stretched the mark with Lazio, and seemed determined to show them he was committed to them. He travelled to Milan with the team, even though he was unfit to play in the away match against Inter. Lazio lost 2–0, and Europe seemed to disappear as the Eagle, Lazio's club symbol, slipped off its perch.

The Mel Stein Louisiana affair was reaching its peak, and rumours of a request for his extradition started to circulate.There had been a congressional hearing about Anglo-American and Carlos Miro and it was big news. He had been telling the United States Authorities that Mel had been involved in all the dodgy dealings. However, as Miro was later sent to prison his testimoney is hardly the most reliable.

Back in the bosom of his Lazio family, Gazza seemed quite relaxed and went to the Italian tennis open several times, being photographed on one occasion sitting near a very beautiful blonde, unfortunately unknown to him.

Dino Zoff took the team away to the hotel, a day earlier than normal before the Ancona match. No-one expected Gazza to play, but club doctor Claudio Bartolini had a special carbon fibre mask designed for him, and he came out onto the pitch looking like the Phantom of the Opera. It worked, the team played well, Gazza was magic and Lazio won 5–0, with goals coming from Cravero, Fuser, Riedle and two from the prolific Signori, who was still at the head of the leading goalscorers table. Europe looked back on target.

The day after the Ancona triumph, the Lazio Stars club had its annual dinner, at which Sergio Cragnotti and the entire Lazio management are always present. This year was no different, and the players were also there to collect awards. Gazza won a special award for his courageous fight back and the magic moments he had contributed to the team. In true Gazza style, when invited by Italian comic actor Enrico Montesano to sing with him, he stood up and sang a few lines from 'The tracks of my tears'. It was a fitting song to sing, as behind the clown's face, the tears and traumas were never far away. It was a magnificently well organized evening, with video clips and presentations to equal a Hollywood gala night. I've never known an English club organize anything to such a high standard. It was a tribute to the enthusiasm and affection of the fans for their club and for all the other sporting clubs in the region of Lazio. Rosaria Romani, chairman of the Lazio stars club said this about Gazza: 'If this year Gazza hasn't been able to give his maximum due to the terrible injury he received, then he has demonstrated that he is a true team leader. I'm sure that next year he will give us the joy of winning something, that we Lazio fans have been waiting so long for.'

Lazio flopped the next week away to Brescia, a game played on neutral territory in Trieste as Brescia had been penalized for crowd trouble. They needed to win what should have been an easy match to qualify for Europe, but they didn't and Gascoigne did not have one of his best matches. After the great performance of last week, he drifted away after a few magic touches in the first half.

England had two vital World Cup qualifying matches approaching, and Gazza went to join his team-mates in England before flying to Poland, and then Norway. As we all know, it was a disaster. England played badly in Poland, scraping a 1–1 draw, through a goal by Ian Wright after Gazza was substituted. Graham Taylor, under enormous pressure and frustrated by his temperamental star, started to hint at the problems that had befallen him with Gazza during the-season as England had tried to qualify for the 1994 World Cup. Having had close contact with Graham, I knew this was born out of frustration, rather than malice.

Gazza's family were furious when they read all the press

reports in which Taylor had accused Gascoigne of being unfit, and overweight. They were extremely worried about Paul. They said that everyone knew he threw up to control his weight and that he also took laxatives to lose weight, so although not overweight, he was simply weakened by the abuse on his body. As one of them put it, 'He just shits all the vitamins out of his body.' No-one knew how to get him to seek professional help. Maybe he had to be shocked into it so that he would face up to his situation and not throw away his natural talent.

The 2–0 disaster against Norway exacerbated a bad situation. Graham Taylor would have been better dropping Gazza but as he said to me on Friday 4 June, 'If it hadn't been Gazza, then everyone would have been shouting for him not to play, but you can't drop Gazza without giving a good reason.' And the reason was that the lad had serious problems, the booze and his behavioural quirks were just symptoms of a much deeper problem which would go back to his childhood. (Graham had told me in an incredulous tone of voice, 'He was in the *sauna* the day of the Norway match trying to lose weight!') The inability to handle the star status, the hatred and fear of being in the public eye had produced a man who found it difficult to cope with his superstar life style. His incredible talent had also brought him deep pain. The distancing from his family had been a negative part of his transformation, the loss of the Roeders had also been tragic and the rise of the influence of Sheryl Kyle had upset his family and caused problems as he had to reconcile his love for her against her hatred for football. It was time to face up to the future and get fit again, both mentally and physically. Whilst away with England Gazza celebrated his 26th birthday. Glenn Roeder says, 'The years between 26 and 29 should be the best for a footballer, there should be a perfect combination of fitness and experience. That is as long as you lead a normal life.'

Graham felt let down by Gazza after he had done everything to give him the support he needs. No other player had been given such special treatment as Gazza. Both Graham and Lawrie have given up weekends to travel to Rome and listen to him, or meet the Lazio officials. The whole England game was built round him. As Graham Taylor says, 'You try and look after him, you try and support him in his quest for fitness but…', his voice trails away. Graham was having his own problems, with the British and Italian press annihilating him. The *Sun* had been particularly vitriolic with the headline 'Who does worse for England?' with a picture of Graham Taylor alongside one of John Major. Graham had fuelled further speculation when he had said, 'If I told you everything about Gascoigne, all hell would break loose.'

On the 30 May in a sun-drenched Olympic Stadium, Lazio beat Napoli 4–3 and earned a place in Europe after a sixteen-year absence. Gazza hadn't been there as he was on England duty, but even without their inspirational player Lazio had shown great determination. There is nowhere like Italy for passion and glory, and the Olympic stadium was aspecial place to be that afternoon. The awful bombing of the Uffizzi gallery in Florence had shocked the country, and in a sign of solidarity, the fans all waved thousands of purple flags, the colours of Fiorentina, as the teams emerged from the tunnel, and there was a minute's silence. At half-time the score was 3–1 to Lazio, and everyone was keeping their fingers crossed. The passion on Cragnotti's face was evident. The fans sang the Lazio hymn at full volume, 'Vola, Lazio, Vola' or 'Fly, Lazio, Fly', and it seemed as if the team was responding to their wishes. In a heartstopping second half, Napoli made a spirited comeback, but Lazio in a show of Gazzalike determination held on to the final whistle. They were back in Europe and they had the Italian league's top goalscorer in Beppe Signori.

At last, after so many barren years things looked good again for Lazio. The question was, would Gazza look good next year? The fans were happy that the team was finally back in Europe. They were delighted to have Gazza amongst them and even though he had experienced an up and down year, they were pleased with his contribution.

Anna Cervelli, who is a great Lazio fan as well as owner of Fintur, producer of sports merchandise, says 'I was very happy when I knew Gazza would be playing for Lazio. After his serious injury, we were all afraid he would never play top level football again, but he's come back and we have all been happy with what he has done for Lazio, even though he wasn't in top physical condition. He has courage and he knows how to transmit this to his team-mates. Obviously, next year, we expect a lot more, because he is a champion, and like all champions he must help Lazio to make the leap in terms of class that we need, to be able to compete with teams like AC Milan. We have waited a long time for this and with Gazza we are sure we will get it.'

Vincenzo Pucci, chairman of Lazio club LC Rignano Flaminio said in the Italian press after Gazza's great performance against Atalanta: 'He's the true difference (in the team). One saw a great Gascoigne, and already I am thinking of next season when he will be the true Gazza, fully recovered and perfectly settled in. He is as important for us as Rivera was for Milan, Platini for Juventus and Falcao for Roma.'

For Gazza, the season had been one of settling in. Never had one player been given such sympathy and support from club and fans alike. But now the joking had to stop and the winning had to start.

POLES APART

W hat of the future? Can we look into our crystal ball and predict what next year will bring for Gazza? From 10 February 1994, it will be the Year of the Dog in the Chinese horoscope and this is what Theodora Lau's *Handbook of Chinese Horoscopes* has to say:

'A distressing year for the Sheep as he has to deal with unhappy changes, debts, romantic problems or family troubles. Not a good time for him to travel or make investments or long term commitments. He must retain an optimistic but very conservative outlook.'

Poor Gazza, could this mean he will have problems with someone running off with his money and infuriating his family? As far as competing in Europe with Lazio is concerned, after February would he be better off staying in bed, and letting the others play for him? Perhaps it's time for him to check up on what has happened to his investments, and to be wary of making any long-term commitments. Somehow, through all this, Gazza has to remain optimistic.

Lazio, up until now, have displayed remarkable patience and understanding towards the player who they hope will lead them towards great victories, but playtime is over.

'I expected a lot from Gascoigne,' said Dino Zoff. 'I expect a lot from him, and he has given a lot. I knew he was coming back after a long lay off due to injury, therefore I knew that he wouldn't give a consistent performance throughout the season. I was aware that he needed time to settle down.'

Next season, however, would be different. 'Next year I expect a Gascoigne who will be in top form and give an outstanding performance. We know that he has the ability, now we need to see consistency.'

When Gazza learnt that Dino Zoff expected another type of music next year, he commented that he would buy him an organ. But it won't be that easy. Dino Zoff was disappointed with Gazza reporting back overweight and unfit on 16 July. The team doctor, Claudio Bartolini, said resignedly, 'Oh well, he was like it *last* year. He reacts quickly to a diet, I expect he'll bounce back.' Zoff said, 'True, he's a bit fat, but I won't make a big thing of it. I had expected better. He has 11 months of hard work ahead of him.' Lazio have defended Gascoigne to the last. Sergio Cragnotti on more than one occasion has said, 'We are building the team round Gascoigne, we expect him to be a leader.'

In an interview with *Il Corriere dello Sport*, Cragnotti said 'When he's given us his all on the pitch, he has enthralled us, therefore he knows how to do it and can do it. We are basing our programme of growth round him. Graham Taylor's insinuations don't affect us. Gazza has great virtues that we have already seen, it doesn't work with the England national team because the England team re-awakens the old vices in him; but you will see Gazza is ours and he will give Lazio great satisfaction.'

No other Italian team has ever displayed such love and affection to a player, and Gazza has been very lucky to have Lazio behind him all the way. But apart from consistency Gazza also needs to grow up. As Terry Venables said when I asked him what could make Gazza happy, 'The security of knowing people are on his side and won't let him down. But he has to work at it, part of growing up is to know who you can rely on and stick with them.'

Gazza remains attached to Terry. When Spurs chairman, Alan Sugar announced that he would like to bring Gascoigne back to Spurs, after Terry had departed from the club, Gazza quickly retorted that he would never return if Terry wasn't at Tottenham.

Many of his friends in England have proved they are reliable and care about him: Terry Venables, John Sheridan, his entire family including his brother-in-law John Paul King, John Coberman, and Glenn and Faith Roeder. But you can't just pick them up and put them down at will, like any relationship. Friendship needs to be worked at, its a two-way thing, and its not enough just to seek out people when you have a problem.

As for football agents, I have always said that the PFA, run by Gordon Taylor, should draw up a manual of simple guidelines for the players. The problem is, most of these lads are now worth a fortune, both for their talent and for the people advising them, and they must be protected. I would suggest these guidelines incorporate explanations of hourly rates for legal/financial advice, differentiation between 'fees' and 'percentages', contractual details and obligations including foreign contracts, where to get independent advice, and a list of 'approved' agents, solicitors and accountants.

Paul's family remain worried about their wayward son. His Mum and Dad were deeply hurt when they read in the Sunday papers that Gazza had gone off to Florida with Sheryl's parents. John Gascoigne was especially disappointed about how Sheryl, encouraged by her father Richard, got Paul to buy her and the kids a house to live in. He didn't like the attitude employed by her father.

What of Sheryl Kyle? Will she stay or will she go? Paul is completely besotted by her, but next year Lazio expect a lot from him and he will have to concentrate on becoming a more consistent performer. Sheryl will have to take a back seat. Yet she is not the type to do that, so something will have to give.

Taylor will be over to see Lazio during the pre-season to sort out the year's programme. I would imagine that if he sees a fit Gascoigne, he will give him another chance in September, but if he has to go through hell with him, then he won't take the risk again. As Graham says, Paul's fitness is better at the beginning of the season and tends to trail off towards the end, so there is a good chance of him appearing against Poland in September. Lawrie McMenemy was watching Gazza at the Makita Tournament in early August to see what shape he was in. A national team is not like a club team, you can't allow a player to suffer from inconsistency or disrupt the preparation time. If it means sacrificing Gascoigne, then Taylor will do it. Inspite of all the criticism Taylor remains true to his word and in excellent rapport with Lazio.

Gazza is generally a very popular person in the dressing room; his jokes always manage to provide a laugh and ease the tension in difficult moments. The foreign players will all be competing for a place in the team. Karlheinz Riedle, the likable German, who scored a hat-trick in the US '93 Cup, was transferred to Borussia Dortmund in the close season for £4.5 million. Lazio have since replaced him with Marseille striker, Alen Boksic, for whom they paid almost £8 million.

Thomas Doll is recovering from a knee injury and is determined to show his exceptional skills on the pitch with Lazio. Aron Winter is indispensable, and his presence is necessary if Lazio are going to bring a cup home. Gazza has to prove he's worthy of a place, which he is if he puts his mind to it.

The move away from his old haunts and friends will one day leave him in the wilderness. Gazza can enthral us with his skills, brighten our day with his jokes, but can he reconcile himself with the unsure, timid boy inside the man? Next season we should see the best of Gazza. Injury apart, he should be mature enough to use his skills intelligently. Can he rise to the occasion, or will it all end in tears?

I hope Gazza comes back and sets the world alight again. He may have driven me mad sometimes, but I remain very fond of him. Not many people could have got away with as much as he has, and still have the world on their side. If he has learnt anything, it will be to use this to his advantage. He needs to put his personal problems behind him get close to friends and family and set about entertaining the fans once again with his magical skills. As Lazio chairman Sergio Cragnotti says, 'He's enthralled us, so we know he can do it.'

Yes, Gazza, we know you can do it, now prove to us that you want to do it.

INDEX